MUAY THAI KICKBOXING

The Ultimate Guide to Conditioning, Training, and Fighting

PALADIN PRESS · BOULDER, COLORADO

CHAD BOYKIN

This book is dedicated to my wife, Tara Lynn Romano,
for her love, strength, beauty, and patience.

Muay Thai Kickboxing:
The Ultimate Guide to Conditioning, Training, and Fighting
by Chad Boykin

Copyright © 2002 by Chad Boykin

ISBN 1-58160-320-7
Printed in the United States of America

Published by Paladin Press, a division of
Paladin Enterprises, Inc.
Gunbarrel Tech Center
7077 Winchester Circle
Boulder, Colorado 80301 USA
+1.303.443.7250

Direct inquiries and/or orders to the above address.

PALADIN, PALADIN PRESS, and the "horse head" design
are trademarks belonging to Paladin Enterprises and
registered in United States Patent and Trademark Office.

Visit our Web site at www.paladin-press.com

Contents

Acknowledgments

First I want to thank my dad, Bobby Boykin, for shooting all of the instructional photos that appear in this book. Thanks for taking the time and having the patience to do everything right.

Thanks to my mom, whose eternal, unconditional, and steady support has given me strength through the years. Donna Boykin worked hard to pass on to me all of her virtues and kindness. But there's only so much one person can do...

Thanks to my big sister, Lisa, for looking out for her baby brother all those years.

Thanks to Granny, Chuck, and all the close family both down south and up north.

I would like to thank Kathy Wirtes and Sue Scott for their work in editing this book. Thanks to Van Carpenter for the equipment assistance. Thanks to Tara Romano, Tony Avery, Mike Walley, Neal Weaver, and Gene Wright for appearing in the photos. Thanks to Brad Donovan for the foreword, and to Billy Dowey, Geoff Balme, and Frank Mullis of Triangle Brazilian Jiu-Jitsu for letting me photograph their class for this book.

Also thanks to all the cronies: "Dirty Work" Andre Carson, the Caveman, Jason Carroll, Dean Scott, Paul Brymer, Glenn Page, Erika Bartolucci, Keri Glover, Jeff Kearney, D.D.S, Brian Mingia, Michelle Rivera, Scott Craddock, Chris Weaver, Chris Webster, Alex Spyrou, Paula Trantham, Mike Bergman, Shane Daughtry, and our late friend, Mike Dean.

Thanks to Doug Ward at Ringside for the photos and hand-wrapping instructions. Thanks to Jon Ford and everyone at Paladin Press for taking a chance on this book.

Warning

Thai boxing, weight training, and contact sports in general guarantee you a serious injury of some kind if you don't display enough intelligence to seek out a competent coach and take basic safety precautions. The list of potential injuries involved in training and competing include brain damage, paralysis, broken bones, heat stroke, heart attack, nerve damage, muscle and ligament damage, internal injuries, blindness, and death. Consult a physician before attempting any exercise program. Neither the author nor the publisher assumes any responsibility whatsoever for the use or misuse of any information contained in this book.

Foreword

During the summer of 1999, I experienced serious health difficulties for the first time in my life. By fall I had undergone surgery, also a first, and by the time it was all over I discovered that at age 46 I had lost that feeling of immortality that most of us grow up with. I began to search for some method of increasing at least the possibility of longevity. I had not participated in any form of real exercise in years, and though I didn't consider myself overweight (190 at 5'10"? That's just my wife's good cooking!), I figured I could use some help trimming up.

I had tried various forms of exercise over the years: jogging, the occasional push-up or sit-up, and mowing the lawn once a week. I even joined a juice-bar health club for a year (I think I actually went four or five times). Nothing but the lawn mowing ever developed into anything close to a regular program, and that went by the wayside every winter.

At a loss for any better ideas, I contacted a friend who had been extolling the virtues of kickboxing to me at every opportunity. My first reaction was predictable . . . I am not a fighter and never have been. (My sole attempt at boxing occurred at approximately age 9, and I don't recall the incident as being very successful.) However, at my friend's urging I eventually found myself at the mercy of the

author of this book. That was in October 1999. With the exception of a month of downtime (my body rebelled at first and required a few weeks of rest and repair), I have been participating in the program offered in these pages between two and three times per week, and have become as ardent a fan of this method of exercise as any of my gym mates.

As I know from my own experience, the idea of becoming involved with "kickboxing" presents a hurdle from its first mention. Most people aren't fighters, and the thought of being pounded to a pulp by those who are is not appealing. My response after 18 months of participation is twofold. First, you don't have to fight to take advantage of the program. I still don't consider myself a fighter by any means; the exercises stand on their own without the need for fist-to-face or shin-to-shin contact. Second, should you get up the nerve to try it, it has been my experience that participating in occasional sparring is actually fun! I have yet to meet someone who is trying to hurt his or her sparring partner, and putting to use the skills learned is more of a lesson in concentration and coordination than it is an effort at uncontrolled mayhem. Besides, even if you never plan to get into a real fight (and I know I don't), the idea that you could, if necessary, is a great confidence builder. Actually, I think it is the sparring that in many ways has maintained my interest and kept me coming back; however, that is not the only thing.

The exercises themselves have done wonders for me, both physically and mentally. I have lost about 20 pounds and at least three inches around my waist, but that's only part of it. At my annual physical recently, every one of the telltale signs doctors use to scare a person into changing their ways showed improvement from my last visit. Not a lot, but by at least a few points: higher good cholesterol and lower bad, better heart rate, better blood count of whatever it is they count, etc. I have changed nothing in my habits or lifestyle beyond the two to three hours a week I devote to the method in this book, and by all measures I appear to have improved my general health appreciably. Again, not the only reason to try this program, but certainly a good one.

Lastly, I would like to say a short word about the author of this book, Chad Boykin. He is one of the biggest reasons that I continue to put myself through the regimen contained in the following pages. Not only has he achieved great success as a fighter, but also he has devoted a great deal of time to the study of exercises and their physiological and psychological effect on the practitioner. His training method pushes me to a level well beyond anything I would ever accomplish on my own, but it is always done in a spirit of goodwill and concern for my personal growth and well-being. I believe that I am now in the best shape of my adult life, and I owe my health and physical confidence in large part to Chad. Try the programs he has put together within this book. With any luck and some hard work, you may end up owing him, too.

—Brad Donovan, 2001

Introduction

The study of almost any martial art holds some kind of positive benefits, including self-discipline, flexibility, stress-relief, and the feeling that one is part of something. It is vitally important, however, that everyone understands that what they are learning may not be of any use.

I have spent the last several years of my life training in boxing, Muay Thai, and recently Brazilian jiu-jitsu. I have had more than 15 fights in the ring and done hours of hard sparring and training for the ring with fighters. I have been teaching kickboxing/Muay Thai for many years. I enjoy sharing what I know about how to fight, which I think is vitally important for empowering everyone who wants to enjoy overall well-being and confidence.

I have discovered through encounters with many people who begin training that the idea of violence is disturbing. Many people think that if they just don't think about it won't ever happen. A natural response is denial; I all too often hear from women, "Oh, I'll never get in a fight." No female *expects* a date rape or a partner that turns physically abusive, but these things happen every day. There are safe houses for battered women right here in my city, with volunteers to help these people pick up the pieces of their lives. The broken bones, lacerations, burns, emotional trauma, and constant fear these

women live with are all real, as is the possibility that they will be murdered. It happens to women of all races and social standings.

Even after the wake-up call of September 11, 2001, we still so want to believe that violence won't happen to us that we avoid thinking about it or preparing to protect ourselves. Well, while I don't ever *want* to have my neck broken in a car crash, that doesn't mean that I can absolutely prevent getting in an accident; thus, I wear a seat belt. Training is like wearing a seatbelt—you may never need it but, if you ever do, it can mean the difference between life and death. And unlike many martial arts instructors, I do not lie to impressionable people and tell them that they will be able to fight anyone, anytime, and come out OK. Training will increase your chances of success but it will not guarantee them. Just like a seatbelt.

There are several martial arts that receive abundant press. If you do not follow the arts then you wouldn't know one from the other. Thank God that the press, and especially Hollywood, is there to inform us. A 120-pound female who won't lift weights because society has convinced her to look like a Q-tip and be "fashionably thin" can knock out a 200-pound bad guy with a spinning whirly-twirl karate kick to his head. It must be true if it's in the movies, right? *Wrong.*

Well then, what effective means of self-defense *should* people learn? There are three methods of fighting that actually provide an effective and efficient means of hurting someone: Muay Thai kickboxing, Brazilian jiu-jitsu, and boxing. This has been proven in a sport that, because of public ignorance and political muscle, has been banned in some states. NHB (no holds barred) or Ultimate Fighting is an anything-goes fight between two well-trained and willing athletes. To date, no one has ever been killed in such an event either at the grassroots or national level. The same is not true for football, pro-wrestling, soccer, or skiing. The evolution of this sport has all but buried traditional striking arts such as the ones receiving so much press lately because these NHB fighters have learned that the only way to win is to do only what works.

The point here is not just to make a case for the sport of NHB. It will never have mainstream acceptance. Violence is disturbing. Unfortunately, as many now realize, it is sometimes unavoidable. The point is to enlighten everyone who is really interested in some little known facts.

In recent months I have seen numerous articles exposing the benefits of various martial arts. Many of these teach worthless fluff, such as punching someone's feet if they are standing over you, or screaming at the bad guy to "scare him away." One article even suggested a "windmilling arms" technique for self-defense on an airplane! This is something I would expect to see from Barney Fife on *The Andy Griffith Show*! If a steroid-using 250-pound monster in the UFC doesn't try flashy TKD kicks and "windmilling arms," what the hell makes a 120-pound female think that it will work for her? The answer is: an uninformed media, Hollywood, and irresponsible instructors.

Every instructor out there is a champion these days. Many martial arts have tournaments that impose very limiting rules regarding contact. For example, striking only to the body, or not making contact at all in point sparring tournaments is common. This is fine, until we have thousands of "champion kickboxers" who have never been in a fight in

their lives decide to teach others! In the NHB there are no limiting rules regarding striking, takedowns, chokes, or joint locks. You see the leg kick, and knee, and elbow strikes of Muay Thai (the national sport of Thailand) in this contest. NHB fighters also utilize the effective punches of boxing and the takedowns and joint locks/chokes of wrestling and Brazilian jiu-jitsu (developed by the Gracie family of Brazil). Why have we not heard of these arts in the mainstream news?

Simple: These arts are violent and scary instead of pretty like the ballet-like choreography brought to us by the majority of "martial arts" whose sole purpose is to sell their programs and "secret techniques" to the wide-eyed children of soccer moms everywhere. So many of these martial arts techniques work only in class with a willing accomplice who knows exactly what to do; the real world just doesn't work that way. They took out the "martial" and shined up the "art" in order to mass market their product to us, the complacent Americans. That is fine, if you accept it for what it is.

Unfortunately, nonaggressive defense philosophies and preplanned techniques that involve a willing accomplice are useless in a real violent situation. But these concepts make us yuppies feel good. We can think, "Yes, I can defend myself and not have to hurt someone. I can learn real self-defense and not have any discomfort other than a little sweat." Look at the old aerobic kickboxing ads where a woman tells us, "Nobody better mess with me now" after punching the air and dancing around to moves more choreographed than a boy-band music video! These people are not living in the real world.

It is unfortunate, but if you really want to be able to defend yourself, a certain level of physical contact and occasional discomfort is absolutely necessary. You want to learn self-defense? Then learn to use your body as a weapon as with Muay Thai, boxing and Brazilian jiu-jitsu (and while you're at it, buy a gun and learn to use it responsibly).

These words may be unsettling to many but I feel the truth must be told. And that is what the free press is all about, right?

KICKBOXING BASICS

Kickboxing comes in many forms. It is a sport, an exercise routine, and a means of self-defense. Kickboxing for exercise purposes became very popular in the late 1990s, mixing (or mutating) various punches from boxing and kicks from karate into an aerobics routine. This activity provides a means of gaining aerobic fitness, but unfortunately is not a reasonable means of learning to defend one's self.

Kickboxing as a sport has four basic styles: American, International, K-1, and Muay Thai.

- American-style kickboxing outlaws kicks to the leg and requires its fighters to throw eight kicks per round.
- International style allows kicks to the leg along with punches.
- K-1 rules allow kicks to the leg, clenching, and knees to the body only.
- Muay Thai allows full-power striking with all of the body's weapons, including fists, shins, feet, knees, and elbows.

This book focuses on Muay Thai-style kickboxing because of its effectiveness. Muay Thai, or Thai boxing, is a devastating striking art developed centuries ago in Thailand. Muay Thai was designed for use in violent confrontation. The originators of this art were the ancient Thai warriors who tested its effectiveness on the battlefield and, years later, in the ring. Today, the Royal Thai Army, as well as U.S. Navy SEAL teams and members of the CIA, use it in unarmed combat training. In addition, it is the national sport of Thailand, with the same level of public interest and enthusiasm as basketball or football in the United States.

There are four major strikes used in the Thai boxing arsenal: punches, knees, elbows, and kicks, along with some use of standing wrestling and throws. All of the body's natural tools are utilized to create an effective and efficient weapon.

Two fighters compete in Muay Thai, the national sport of Thailand. Photo by Zoran Rebac, from his book Thai Boxing Dynamite *(Paladin Press).*

As the shins are gradually hardened with kicks on the bag, they become club-like weapons to be used in conjunction with the hands, elbows, and knees. In Thailand, most males at one time or another learn the skills of traditional Muay Thai, either for sport or recreation.

There are many martial arts practiced around the world; striking arts like karate, taekwon do, and kung fu are commercially popular in the United States and can provide many benefits to the practitioner. However, if the point of training in martial arts is to learn effective stand-up self-defense regardless of size and natural athletic ability, then Muay Thai stands alone. The Thai system of self-defense and the conditioning required for its success are unparalleled in effectiveness for people of all sizes.

History shows that Muay Thai has dominated all of its challengers in the ring and battlefield with stunning efficiency. It is not that the individual punches, kicks, or knee and elbow strikes themselves possess any magic; the success lies in its realistic approach and the conditioning required during training. Knowledge and experience are attained through contact sparring and hitting the pads and bags with full power.

Traditional martial-arts displays—such as smashing bricks, wood, and other inanimate objects—may be impressive feats of power and skill. However, with Muay Thai there is a living, breathing opponent moving and hitting you back! Fighting in the ring is a supreme challenge of will and determination, not simply a graceful display of athleticism and concentration. Muay Thai, for example, does not require the practice of *katas*, or forms. Katas are choreographed movements that are memorized by practitioners of most other stand-up martial arts. There is no substitute for the realism found in Muay Thai training, be it for serious competitors or recreational athletes.

The colored-belt system of promotion prevalent in most martial arts began with Jigoro Kano (known as the father of judo) as a means of testing a student's knowledge of a particular art. Thai boxers train for championship title belts, which they will fight for in stadiums and arenas around the world. But as Muay Thai's popularity grows there are more and more people who wish to train and learn it, but do not aspire to compete as fighters in the ring. For them a system of increasingly more demanding tests can be established to provide a means of showing progress in the application of the techniques and in physical conditioning. These tests should include physical conditioning, sparring, and fluid application of techniques. Generally the tests will show intermediate, advanced, and instructor levels of ability.

There are many anecdotes that establish Muay Thai as a viable means of fighting in self-defense situations. One incident that was published in every Bangkok newspaper years ago is such a testimony to Muay Thai's effectiveness in the street. A young man on his way home was surrounded by a group of robbers that were notorious for terrorizing travelers in the Bangkok suburbs. Unarmed, he defended himself, giving two of his assailants trips to the hospital with broken ribs, and a third with a broken jaw. Other attackers fled but were apprehended by the police. The courageous man was a local Thai boxer, who escaped the attack with only minor injuries.[1] Of course, no one is invincible, but this kind of story should not be taken for granted; it is a testimony to the value of regular training.

It is not necessary for someone to want to enter the ring or NHB arena to benefit from learning the techniques. Each year thousands of everyday people seek out Muay Thai training, not only as a positive outlet for stress and aggression, but also to help develop confidence, cardiovascular fitness, muscular strength, self-defense skills, coordination, agility, and balance. There is also a great mutual respect and bond shared by those who train together; you can learn more about a person by spending a few hours in training with them than you can in months of conversation.

The "secrets" of Muay Thai are simply hard work and regular practice. The rewards are priceless. The beauty of the techniques lies in their simplicity; it will not take decades to learn the basics of the art. Within several weeks of regular training, and with qualified instruction, anyone can see noticeable improvements in skill, conditioning, and strength. While this book will illustrate many of the Thai boxing basics, *training under qualified supervision is a must*. A qualified instructor must see and correct important technique flaws. Perfect practice makes perfect.

ORIGINS

Many of the Muay Thai archives were destroyed when the early Thais were at war with the Burmese. The information that we have comes from the writings of Burmese, Cambodian, and early European visitors, as well as some of the chronicles of the Lanna Kingdom in Chiangmai.[2]

The origin of Muay Thai is associated with the migrations of the Thai ("free") tribe in the 12th and 13th centuries from the Juang-Xi, Sichuan, and Hubei provinces south of China into what we know today as Thailand. There is, therefore, some speculation that Thai boxing has some roots in kung fu (Chinese boxing), though styles and training methods vary greatly today.[3] Other sources indicate that Thai boxing originated during the violent battles that took place between the Thai Kingdom and neighboring Burma, Khmer, and Cham (Vietnam).

More than a thousand years ago the Thai warriors documented their fighting strategies and techniques. The information was documented from years of combat from the warrior clans until the clans settled into what is known today as Thailand. This ancient collection of techniques, known as the *Chupasart*, taught fighting with knives, swords, spears, battleaxes, pikes, and crossbows. It became the bible of the warriors and the textbook of fighting skills to the young men trained by the warriors of that country.[4]

Legends say the warriors trained young men using this remarkable manual of armed combat without any weapons. These warriors substituted their limbs for clubs and swords, learning to fight with or without weapons (although I'm sure they preferred being armed). Each part of the body became a weapon and thus, the art of Thai boxing began, and over the centuries evolved from its battlefield combat origins into the fighting sport we know today.

HISTORY

Thai boxing continued to evolve. National disputes were settled using the hand-to-hand combat methods born of Thailand. These fighting techniques were also taught in public schools and used in military training. Thai boxing's rise to national prominence in Thailand came from some incredible historic events.

In the 14th century, King Sen Muang Mu of Thailand died, leaving his two sons Fang Keng and Ji Kumkam to fight for the throne. The conflict escalated as both sides had ardent supporters, and there was a threat of civil war. It was decided that the two factions would fight to decide the future king. The fighter from the Ji Kumkam side prevailed, thus winning him the crown.[5]

A historical document dating back to 1560 describes a duel between Thai Prince Naresuan (known as the Black Prince) and the son of Burma's King Bayinnaung. The duel lasted for several hours and concluded with the death of the Burmese crown prince. The prince was the only successor to the throne and the Burmese decided not to attack Thailand without the guidance of a recognized leader.[6]

In 1767, Lord Mangra, the king of Burma, decided to entertain himself and his country with a seven-day fete celebrating the fact that Burma had all but conquered Thailand. After learning that one of the Thai POWs, Nai Khanom Tom, was considered the best fighter in Thailand, Lord Mangra opted to pit him against his best boxer.[7] Before the fight began, Nai Khanom Tom danced slowly around his opponent in a ritual ceremony known as the *wai kru*, which is still practiced today. The prefight ritual expresses respect, and is also believed to improve a fighter's concentration and focus. The favored Burmese fighter was taken off guard by the odd spectacle unfolding in front of him. When the fight signal was finally given the Thai fighter rushed forward and overwhelmed his adversary, ending the fight in seconds. The officials ruled the knockout illegal, claiming the wai kru had distracted the Burmese fighter. Nai Khanom Tom was immediately ordered to fight nine more Burmese challengers, each determined to kill him. One by one each of the contenders fell unconscious to the flurry of elbows, kicks, and knees. The last challenger, a boxing instructor from Ya Kai City, had his legs and body so badly mangled that no one would challenge the Thai captive again. Lord Mangra was so impressed by the unusual skills of the Thai fighter that he offered Nai Khanom Tom his choice of money or two beautiful wives. Nai Khanom Tom won his freedom and traveled back to his homeland with his two new wives.

By defeating the best Burmese fighters of the day, Nai Khanom Tom became a part of Thai history; an annual tournament is held in his name to this day.

Some 20 years later, two French boxers came to Bangkok and issued a challenge to all Thai fighters, claiming that no Thai boxer could beat them. The Frenchmen's bold challenge led the king to call for fighters willing to defend the honor of their country. Muen Phlaan, a teacher of Thai boxing and wrestling, answered the challenge. For the contest, a pavilion was erected near the western theater of the Temple of the Emerald Buddha, and there was great anticipation for the match. The fight was decidedly one-sided, and both Frenchmen were defeated. These incidents and legends are responsible for introducing the skills of Muay Thai to the outside world.[8]

Late in the 18th century, due largely to a ruler known as the "Tiger King," Thai boxing enjoyed renewed development and recognition. King Pra-Chao Sua was an expert in Muay Thai, but since it was a serious offense to assault a king, he was forced to hide his identity with a mask. The Tiger King would slip out of his palace and don his disguise, and was a regular winner in local tournaments, fighting all comers. During his reign, Thai boxing was at a peak in popularity.[9]

Customs of this early era of fighting included:

- Binding the hands with loosely woven raw cotton threads or strips of horsehair knotted like a seashell at the fingertips. This would give the hand a hard and abrasive surface; in some cases the bound hands would be dipped in glue and sprinkled with finely ground glass.
- Hardening the shins and fists by repeatedly kicking and hitting rubber plants and palm trees. (The rubber plants have been replaced by canvas bags.)
- Protecting the groin by tying half-shell coconuts around the fighter's waist with hemp.
- Tying lemons at two ends of a rope and punching for focus and precision, similar to the way double-end bags are used today.
- Sparring, long-distance running, and some training underwater.

In 1929, the old-style hand bindings were replaced with padded gloves. The use of ground glass on the fists had already been discontinued. Also around this time, five-minute rounds with two-minute rest periods were instituted, along with weight classes and the outlawing of strikes to the groin. Before the introduction of weight classes, a fighter could and did fight all challengers regardless of size and weight. This change meant that the fighters were more evenly matched and instead of there being one champion, there became one for each weight class. Rules were set in place to lower the number of fatalities during fights, to establish a more marketable sport worldwide, and to increase the longevity of the contestants.

TRADITIONS

Many traditions remain in the sport of Muay Thai, including music, a prefight ritual, and nicknaming fighters. These Buddhist traditions are a strong part of the Thai culture, but fighters from other nations sometimes ignore them.

In a Thai setting, an orchestra plays distinctive and rhythmic music that follows the tempo of the fight. The orchestra consists of drums, cymbals, and jawa flutes. As the fight pace picks up or slows down, so does the music.

As mentioned earlier, the old custom of wai kru is an expression of respect. The boxer salutes the crowd with ceremonious bows and sweeping motions with the arms to the head. He then performs a series of slow, spiritual, dance-like movements unique to the individual and the camp that trains him. Besides paying respect, this ritual is designed to bring concentration to the fighter, loosen his body up, relieve anxiety, and rid the ring of bad spirits. (Translated, wai kru means, "getting rid of fear from the heart.") After the performance the fighter goes to his corner and removes his *mongkon*, which is a stiff cord that loops around the head and juts out at the back like the handle on a tennis racket.

The ritual of naming novice fighters according to their temperament, skills, combativeness, and character is also practiced. A fighter's surname is the name of his school and his individual nickname. Common names are tiger, cobra, and dragon, and each fighter symbolizes some of the characteristics of a particular animal, like speed, power, agility, or courage.[10]

MUAY THAI VS. OTHER MARTIAL ARTS

Muay Thai is the most practical method of fighting on your feet in the ring or on the street. The balance, positioning, power, and realism of its training is what makes it so efficient. More commercial and popular stand-up arts such as American karate and taekwon do are much less effective because of the rules and practices of combat that they impose in point sparring matches.

Point sparring diminishes real combat training in several ways. It requires fighters to practice and train with light contact, barely touching each other. Fighters just trying to score points touch their opponents only on the designated areas of their bodies instead of using methods that would win fights or render their attackers helpless. Kicks are thrown high, which is impractical in the street or in a ring fight with open rules (unless set up properly with punches to the face and low kicks). Punches to the head are not thrown, and the combatants are stopped and separated after one fighter scores one point. Lastly, point fighters are taught to pull their punches before they hit their targets.

Sport karate, or kickboxing, popped up in the United States in the late 1970s and created a following. Now martial artists (and boxers) could test their skills in the ring under conditions similar to boxing, with three-minute rounds, full contact, and knockouts. However, American and International kickboxing rules outlaw the use of the knees, elbows, and in many cases, even kicks to the leg!

Most American-style kickboxing matches have a requirement of seven or more above-the-waist kicks per round. It is necessary to institute a minimum number of kicks in a kickboxing match because without this rule, kickboxing would resemble boxing more than anything else! Flashy karate and taekwon do kicks look impressive but are not so effective in the ring; high kicks are useless unless a fighter has his guard completely down, and even then the likelihood of scoring a knockout with punches is much more probable. This is not merely opinion but fact proven in the ring. There have been many fighters from various styles to challenge Muay Thai fighters over the past several decades.

On January 22, 1974, kung fu masters from Hong Kong were all knocked out in the first round against Muay Thai opponents.[11] The legendary matches took place in front of 15,000 spectators at Hua Mark stadium in Bangkok, Thailand. In five fights the fans saw only 6 1/2 minutes of action!

A few months later, a team of Chang Tung stylists from Singapore arrived to fight. Among them was one fighter who had earned the nickname "Black Killer" because he had allegedly killed an opponent in an unofficial tournament. The feared Black Killer was knocked out in the first round, and his comrades all suffered similar defeats in the Thai boxing matches.[12]

In a televised match in Manilla, Philippines, between National Karate Champion Kandido Picate and Thai boxer Nirund Bunjanet, Picate fell twice in the first round and was knocked out in the second.

Other first-round knockouts occurred in 1959. This time the victims were a team of tai kek fighters from Formosa.[13]

Tse Shang, a Chinese martial arts master from the Guandong province had to undergo months of medical treatment, despite a worldwide reputation for his high mastery of "chi" (energy), after losing to Thai boxer Ian Hantaley in 1921.[14]

American kickboxing icon Benny "the Jet" Urquidez lost two Thai boxing bouts in the 1970s, although his record was saved due to the first match being called a "no contest" and the second loss being unpublicized.[15]

In September 1983, famous American kickboxer Don Wilson traveled to Thailand to fight in Rachadamneon Stadium against Thai champion Samaad Prasamit from the Konken province. Despite a weight advantage of nine kilos, Wilson was dropped twice in the five-round bout and lost the decision.[16]

In 1996 in a bout in the United States, a 22-year-old from Chiang Mai Thailand (Sow), knocked out a professional boxer (Murphy) with a left hook to the jaw 30 seconds into the first round despite a 30-pound weight disadvantage. The Thai stylist bombarded the Western boxer with so many

Students practice Brazilian jiu-jitsu with Geoff Balme. This fighting form may be used with Muay Thai in NHB or mixed martial arts.

weapons from all limbs that the boxer had to go on the defensive. The pain weakened his legs and opened him up for a knockout punch—a weapon from his own arsenal![17]

MIXED MARTIAL ARTS COMBAT

For years, martial artists argued over whose styles and theories were superior in "real fighting." In the past several years NHB or mixed martial arts[18] competitions have become the proving ground by allowing combat with little or no rules. Full-power strikes from any part of the body, throws, chokes, and joint locks are all allowed while standing or while fighting on the ground (amateur competitions do not allow strikes to the head while on the ground). Fighters either can be knocked out, submit (tap out), or win by judge's decision. Of course, due to the damage that is possible, a referee is in place to ensure both fighters' safety. While there has been much criticism and persecution by

politicians and other groups whose aim is to ban this sport, it should be noted that no combatant in NHB competition has died, to date, from competition. The same cannot be said for other sports, including such mainstream staples as football and soccer.

The influence of Muay Thai shin kicks, knees, and elbows is evident in NHB competition worldwide. The evolution of Thai boxing continues into the NHB or mixed martial arts arenas, as it has recently been integrated with Brazilian-style jiu-jitsu. This hybrid of styles combines the best stand-up and ground fighting components to form a complete fighting method for self-defense, competition, or recreation.

Recently, NHB fighting has become popular with promotions like UFC (Ultimate Fighting Championship), Extreme Fighting Championship, and hundreds of regional minor promotions hosting mixed martial arts events year-round. Combatants in these tournaments utilize grappling, ground fighting, and striking. Freestyle wrestler Mark Coleman soundly defeated all of his UFC opponents until he faced the kicks, punches, elbows, and grappling of Maurice Smith in UFC XIV for the UFC Superfight Heavyweight Championship. By October 1999, Coleman was training in Muay Thai with Thai trainer, Manu N'toh.[19] The combination of wrestling, Thai boxing, and Brazilian jiu-jitsu by fighters makes for a complete range of abilities. In late 1999, Frank Shamrock (a UFC Champion NHB fighter) said: "Muay Thai is the most brutal of all sports. Hands down it's an entire body wreck every time you go out to fight. I have a lot of respect for those guys. America is behind on the current kickboxing scene. Maurice Smith was kind of an innovator here with the low kick. But (for the most part) we're still in the karate days."[20]

Other NHB fighters who have been successful with Muay Thai techniques include Danny "Boy" Bennett (Muay Thai), Bas Rutten (Muay Thai and Shootfighting), Dave Menne (Muay Thai and Brazilian jiu-jitsu), Marco Ruas (Muay Thai and Vale Tudo), Pele Landi (Muay Thai), Igor Vovchanchin (Muay Thai), Mark Kerr (wrestling/Muay Thai), and many others. The influence of Thai-style kicking, clenching, and knee striking is prevalent in NHB competition worldwide. The stand-up fighting game of this new breed of competitor is rounded out by the punches and footwork influenced by both Western and Thai boxers. A mixing of Muay Thai, Brazilian jiu-jitsu, and weapons training provides a complete system of self-defense, whether it is for competition in NHB or the street.

PROTECTIVE EQUIPMENT

Muay Thai training requires the use of some protective equipment. The necessary safety gear you will need from head to toe includes ankle guards, shinguards, groin protector, Thai shorts, handwraps, gloves, mouthpiece, and headgear.

Handwraps
Because the hand contains many small, delicate bones that are subject to repetitive impact with the force of punching practice, it is essential that everyone learns how to wrap the hands correctly. (Instructions provided by Ringside, Inc.)

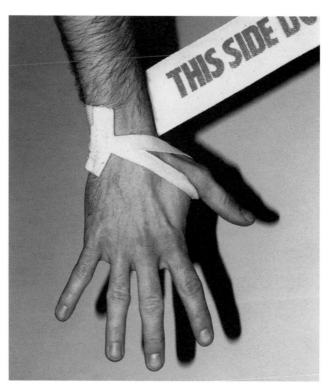

Figure 1: Begin by placing the thumb loop over the thumb. Start wrapping firmly across the back of the hand.

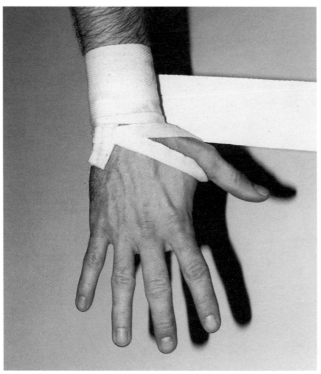

Figure 2: Wrap around the wrist three times for stable wrist support. Overlap just a half-length as you wrap down the wrist.

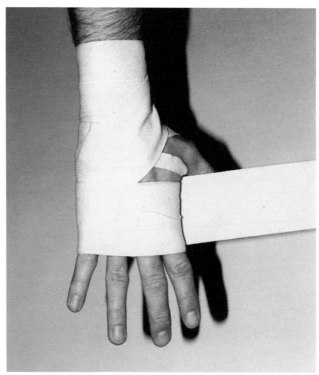

Figure 3: Bring the wrap across the back of the hand and wrap twice around the knuckle area. The edge of the wrap should be about halfway up to the first knuckle of fingers.

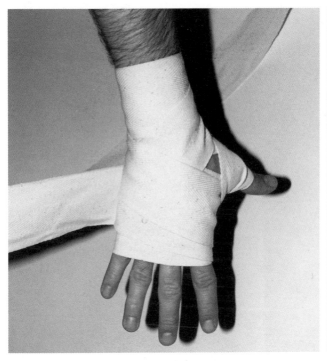

Figure 4: Bring the wrap across the bottom of the hand. Wrap around the thumb, from the bottom around the top of the thumb and then across the palm. Take it around the back of the hand, then over the top of the thumb and around the back of the hand again.

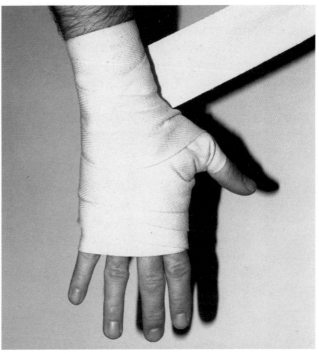

Figure 5: Take the wrap around the wrist and then across the back of the hand. Wrap around the knuckle area again as shown.

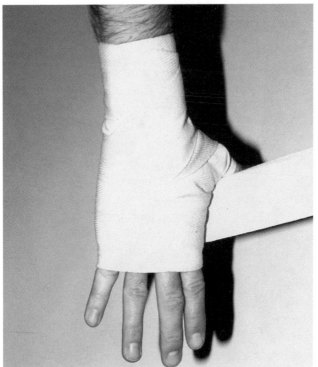

Figure 6: Go back across the top of the hand as shown. This will make an X-pattern on the top of the hand. This pattern is the best for stabilizing the bones of the hand.

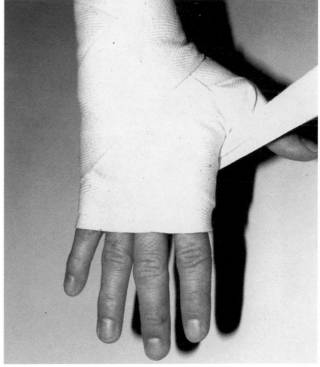

Figure 7: Continue making an X-pattern on the top of the hand. Occasionally go around the knuckles and wrist as illustrated.

Ankle Guards

These are designed to support the delicate ankle joint from the stresses of training. Various manufacturers produce ankle guards made of different materials, most of elastic and rigid cloth or neoprene. It is important to use ankle guards, especially when training barefoot.

Bag gloves are lighter than sparring gloves and are perfect for shadowboxing.

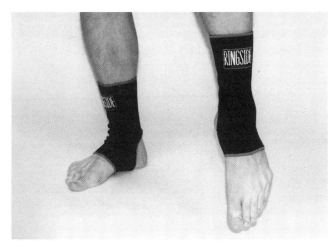

Figure 8: The finished wrap should look like this. It should be snug, but not too tight. If you keep the wrap smooth as you wrap, the wrap will be more comfortable and will not cut off circulation or unravel. Hold the fist as shown with the wrist bent slightly downwards and the fist flat.

Ankle guards are important, especially when training barefoot.

Gloves

Boxing gloves are made to suit different purposes, so features vary.

Bag gloves are lightweight and designed for use when training on the *double-end bag* or for *shadowboxing*. If you are used to training with heavier sparring gloves, you will notice that you have increased punching speed when using this type of glove. Also, the use of bag gloves serves to extend the life of the more expensive and heavier sparring gloves.

Sparring gloves are available from 10-ounce to 18-ounce, and are made of leather, synthetic leather, or vinyl. Regardless of the material, sparring gloves are good for general training

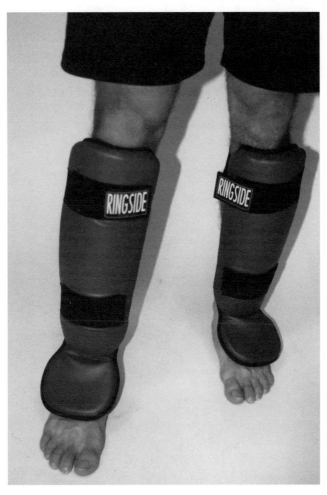

Shin guards are recommended for use during sparring practice, but not while practicing kicks on the bag or Thai pad.

because their weight will help you develop more strength and endurance in your arms and shoulders. For safety you should use at least 14-ounce gloves, as the extra padding will reduce your partner's likelihood of head injury. Gloves can be open or closed thumb and are lace-up, pull-on, or secured with hook and loop.

Shin guards

Shin guards are not recommended for bag or Thai pad kicking practice because they will slow down the conditioning and toughening of the shins. For sparring practice, however, shin guards are important for reducing the likelihood of lower leg injury, as anyone who has ever driven their shin or instep into a training partner's kneecap or elbow can attest to. Some shinguards are made of cloth and pull up the

shin to provide some padding for protection, while others are made of leather and are secured with hook and loop straps. Most provide an instep guard for the top of the foot as well as padding for the shins.

Groin Protector

I will assume that a detailed description for the need of this particular piece of protective equipment is not necessary. The Thais have used steel cups for hundreds of years; however, plastic ones are now available. Some made for boxing also have cushioning for the lower abdomen. Needless to say, this is a must for sparring, regardless of your experience level.

Mouthpiece

This also is a must for sparring. Mouthpieces come in single or double guard (to protect both the upper and lower teeth), and are made of plastic or rubber. Recent advances in the design of certain professional mouthpieces allow more airflow and jaw joint protection.

All mouthpieces must be fitted properly; follow the directions provided with the gear.

Thai Shorts

These shorts are made of nylon or satin and can be custom made with a variety of designs, school names, or logos. The Thais have custom made these shorts for centuries to allow plenty of leg room for high kicks and elastic waistbands for a snug fit at the waist. The Thai shorts dry quickly and do not hold moisture and sweat like cotton. They keep you cool when training in hot weather, and also make comfortable shorts for running. Many have Thai writing and designs across the front. The color of the shorts represents different levels of experience and skill in Thailand, with red shorts being the most sought after.

Headgear

For sparring practice, a good set of headgear is highly recommended to lessen the chance of head injuries. Sparring with control provides the best protection, but even then accidents do happen, so it is important to be prepared. Headgear comes in many styles, some with face

Thai shorts are loose to allow for high kicks. This pair has the Thai word for Muay Thai emblazoned on the front.

guards to protect the nose. Remember, an ounce of prevention is worth a pound of cure.

•••

1. World Muay Thai Council: <www.wmtc.nu/index.html>
2. ibid.
3. Rebac, Zoran. *Thai Boxing Dynamite: The Explosive Art of Muay Thai.* Boulder, CO: Paladin Press, 1987.
4. World Muay Thai Council.
5. Rebac.
6. ibid.
7. Carter, Dave. "Tradition: The Heart of Muay Thai." *Muay Thai.* Burbank: CFW Enterprises. April 2000.
8. World Muay Thai Council.
9. ibid.
10. Rebac.
11. Praditbatuga, Pop. The Belt is in the Ring, <http://members.aol.com/Thaiboxing2000/muay.html>
12. Rebac.
13. ibid.
14. ibid.
15. Wayne, C. Journal of Chinese Martial Science, <http://members.tripod.com/~crane69/index6d.htm>
16. ibid.
17. Praditbatuga.
18. NHB and mixed martial arts are one and the same—a new version of a sport that dates back to ancient Greece. The roots of mixed martial arts, boxing, Greco-Roman, and professional wrestling lie in this combat sport called Pancration. The ancient Greeks used strikes, takedowns, wrestling, and submission holds in the Pancration match.
19. Praditbatuga.
20. Quadros, Stephen. "What Does it Take to Win the K-1?" *Inside Kung Fu* (November 1999): p. 118.

MUAY THAI TERMS

Cultural Terms

Acharn: Teacher
Chai: Yes
Ching: Percussion instrument
Glawng khaek: Drum
Kai: School
Korb khun krup: Thank you
Kru: Teacher
Mai chai: No
Mongkon: Headband
Pah pra jiad: Armbands
Pi: Reedy Flute
Ram muay: A dance unique to each fighter that is performed at the end of the wai kru.
Sa wad dee krup: A greeting. Used when meeting and leaving; means "to be prosperous."
Wai: Bow
Wai kru: A ceremony performed before a fight to pay respect to everyone the fighter wishes to honor, which could include the fighter's parents, teachers, fellow fighters, the king of Thailand, and Buddha.
Wat: Monastery

Fighting Terms

Bung: Block
Buok: Shin block (leg check)
Chok: Punch (the jab, right cross, etc.)
Djog yan: "Piercing a pair of bellows." Used when describing the trademark leg kick.
Fet rao: Knockout
Kao: Knee
Mat aat: Uppercut
Mat tong: Hook punch
Rook: Advance
Sok: Elbow
Tad Mara: Throw
Tarng Pa: Elbow chop
Te: Round kick
Teep: Push kick (foot jab)
Thum: A throw
Tiip: Straight kick (includes both front and side kicks)
Toi: Retreat
Yaek: Break
Yud: Stop

Thai Numbering System

1 = **Nung**
2 = **Sorng**
3 = **Sam**
4 = **See**
5 = **Ha**
6 = **Hok**
7 = **Jet**
8 = **Paed**
9 = **Gaow**
10 = **Sip**

CHAPTER 2
Strikes and Defenses

This chapter provides written descriptions and illustrations of the basic Muay Thai strikes; all the weapons—the knee, elbow, fists, shins, and feet—are described. Study them carefully and if possible find a qualified instructor in Muay Thai or mixed martial arts to ensure that your form is correct. These chapters can serve as an excellent reference but cannot substitute for proper coaching.

The basic defenses in Thai boxing involve either blocking or evading oncoming strikes while maintaining posture and balance. *Evading* a blow is the best defense; it means avoiding the contact by moving the body slightly out of the range of the strike. *Blocking* involves either absorbing the impact of the blow while covering up vital parts of the body (chin, nose, groin, upper leg, stomach) or redirecting the path of the weapon being used to attack.

FIGHTING STANCES AND FOOTWORK

Boxing and Kickboxing Stances

The basic position if you're a right-handed fighter is to stand on the balls of your feet with most of your weight on your back (right) foot. The left foot should be forward and the feet just less than shoulder width apart. In pure boxing the fighter will be standing somewhat sideways to make the head a harder target to punch. With Muay Thai, however, a sideways position is harmful because of the exposed lead leg (remember, boxers are not concerned with having their legs kicked), so keep your body facing forward, with hips straight, and toes pointing slightly out for balance. Keep a little more of your weight on your back leg; too much weight on your lead leg makes receiving a leg kick even more damaging. Muay Thai practitioners also stay on the balls of their feet as part of their footwork, as this makes shifting the bodyweight to the ball of either foot for the round kick very fast, making a more effective and powerful kick.

The Muay Thai position traditionally places the hands in front of the face with the arms somewhat extended, unlike a Western boxing position in which the hands and elbows are tucked in. The reasoning is that, in Thailand, Muay Thai fighters are awarded more points for leg kicks and elbow and knee strikes than for punches. This is due, in part, to the fact that ancient Thai fighters did not wear any gloves. For the sake of developing a safer, more marketable sport, rule modifications were implemented by sanctioning bodies after World War II. These rules included making the boxers wear small, padded gloves in the ring. Since only the hands are padded, punches are considered to be the least important of the strikes by some in the Thai culture. In addition, extended arms

Conventional kickboxing stance with hips square and hands high.

1975 Pan American boxing champ Tony Avery demonstrates a left-handed boxing stance.

would allow opponents to grab fighters in the clench faster than a "hands-in" position.

In order for a boxer to attain full punching power, the hands are kept closer to the face. It should be noted that in recent years as more European fighters have competed in Thailand there has been more use of the punching techniques than in decades past.

In the basic position keep the hands up, chin down, and elbows tucked in close to the body. Hand position can be manipulated depending on the situation; for clenching, keep the hands further out in front of the face, for power punches keep the hands closer to the face. Experience and practice will make you more comfortable in knowing which hand position is best for the situation, and to be versed in both is important.

BASIC FOOTWORK

Footwork is also an essential part of the fighter's foundation of skills, whether you're using a Thai or American boxing position. There are similarities between the two.

Step with the appropriate foot (step with your left foot to go forward and left, your right foot to go backward and right), and slide the opposite foot to cover the distance of the step. Do not cross your feet or bring your feet together after throwing punches—this jeopardizes your balance and is a waste of energy.

Make small, subtle steps to get closer to or farther away from an opponent. Refer to the *square drill* in the following chapter for a good footwork exercise. Also, be aware that lateral movement is a key to success. Do not always move straight ahead; practice moving from side to side as you work an opponent. Movement is always a key to successful self-defense because a moving target is much more difficult to hit than a stationary one. It is important to move outside your opponent's jab (or lead hand) as you work. Move to your right when facing a right-handed fighter and to your left when facing a left-handed fighter.

Shadowboxing

Shadowboxing can be a good general warm-up and serve to improve your footwork skills and concentration through practice. The idea is to "spar" against an imaginary opponent, going through the motions of a fight. Sharp punches, kicks, knees, and elbows are practiced with speed and accuracy in front of a mirror to prepare for training, warm up the body, and get mentally focused. Be aggressive one round, defensive another. Concentrate on your footwork, balance, lateral movement, defense, and striking in combinations for several rounds. This is a staple of Thai and Western boxing warm-ups.

STRIKES: JAB AND CROSS

Jab

The jab is a fundamental offensive and defensive weapon. It sets up more powerful shots (such as low kicks and power punches), keeps your opponent off balance, can be used to dictate the pace of the fight, and can break your opponent's rhythm. For example: A tall boxer may utilize the jab to keep smaller opponents away, while shorter fighters could double the jab as they step in close to take away the reach advantage.

How to: From the basic position take a small step forward. Rotate your hips and left shoulder as you fully extend the left jab. Keep the left elbow down and turn the forearm over so that the palm is down and the first two knuckles land in a level position. After you throw the punch, return immediately to your starting position with both hands up. Don't let the elbow come up or out while throwing the jab. Your punch will make a straight line. Do not lean forward. This will disrupt your balance, reduce the power of your punch, and leave you vulnerable for a countermove.

Warming up with shadowboxing.

Kickboxer Gene Wright demonstrates the left jab.

Right Cross

The right cross is a fundamental power punch because it is thrown with the weight of the entire body behind it. It is often set up with one or two jabs, which hides the cross and distracts the opponent. Many knockouts in the ring come by way of a correctly placed straight right.

How to: From the basic position, begin by driving off the ball of your back foot. Rotate the right hip and shoulder forward and extend the right hand and arm fully. At this point the right shoulder should be closer to the opponent than the left shoulder and the fist should turn over. Keep the right elbow down while turning the forearm over so that the palm is down and the first two knuckles land in a level position. Immediately return to the basic position with both hands up after throwing the cross. Don't let the elbow come up or out while throwing the cross. Do not lean forward at the trunk—this will disrupt your balance, reduce the power of your punch, and leave you vulnerable for a counter move.

DEFENDING AGAINST THE JAB AND CROSS

Keeping your hands in the proper position is essential for blocking both of the straight punches.

Brush (Block)

Keep the right hand in the basic position and wait for the jab to come to you. Simply deflect the punch by pushing it slightly in the same direction that it is going, using the left hand to brush away a right punch and vice versa. Do not let your hand come away from your face or "reach" to block the jab. The right hand only needs to move a couple of inches to brush away the jab; overextension or reaching will leave your face open.

The right cross.

The traditional boxer's brush, brushing the jab with the palm.

Thai-Style Brush (Block)

The Thai-style brush is performed similar to the traditional boxer's brush illustrated above. However, the objective here is to off-balance your opponent in order for you to clench him and knee. Sweep the opponent's punch (on the same side) across your body and down toward your hip, pulling him forward and into a knee or elbow strike. Simultaneously use the other hand to clench his head or neck as he is leaning forward.

Follow the same instructions for the boxer's brush, except that you will "pull" your opponent forward instead of merely deflecting the punch.

Deflect your opponent's jab or cross from in front of your face by moving your same-side hand diagonally across your body and downward to your opposite hip.

The fighters square up in a basic position with their hands high.

This will pull him in closer and disrupt his balance, allowing you to quickly reach straight across and grab his head with your right hand for a knee strike.

Catch (Block)

From the basic position, the jab or cross can be caught in the open palm of the right glove. Be sure to keep resistance and some tension in the arms to avoid hitting yourself. This block requires you to use your hands as a wall of defense.

The catch block.

Elbow Block (Block)

Block a straight jab or cross by bringing your left elbow up and driving the elbow into your opponent's jab hand. From the basic position, imagine you are patting yourself on the back, thus your elbow is raised in the path of the jab. Return your hand back to the starting position immediately.

The elbow block.

Outside Slip (Evasion)

The outside slip involves dropping your torso forward and away from your opponent's centerline, bending a little at the knees and the waist. (Imagine drawing a vertical line straight down your opponent from head to toe—this is his centerline.) You are moving away from your opponent's power side. Do not move your neck and do keep your eyes on your opponent—never look away.

The purpose of the slip is to avoid your opponent's punch without getting out of range for throwing a fast counterpunch. Also, for balance, you want to avoid the blow by the smallest amount of room. Whether you slip to the left or right will be determined by which punch you are slipping. Keep your hands up and in position, as you must be able to counterpunch and block.

The outside slip.

Inside Slip (Evasion)

The inside slip involves dropping the torso forward and into your opponent's centerline, bending a little at the knees and the waist. Your head should end up directly over your left knee. It is not recommended that you slip inside unless you are going to punch immediately, as you are moving directly into your opponent's power side. Do not move your neck and keep your eyes on your opponent—don't look away.

The inside slip.

Fade (Evasion)

The fade is executed by moving the shoulders and head straight back to avoid a straight jab or cross. To use the fade alone is dangerous; it is best used in conjunction with a push kick or knee strike to avoid being "stuck" leaning slightly backwards. Again, for balance, you want to miss getting hit only by the smallest possible fraction.

The fade.

STRIKES: HOOKS

Left Hook

The hook can be a devastating knockout punch and is valuable at close range. The hook takes a while to learn correctly, but it is well worth learning. Many people have been knocked out after throwing a sloppy hook from too far away!

How to: Start close to your opponent; do not attempt to hook from far away. Begin by dipping your right knee slightly and squaring up your hips to the opponent. Transfer your weight to the ball of your lead foot as you start to pivot your hip. Simultaneously bring up your elbow to a horizontal position, parallel to the floor (your arm will now be bent at a 90-degree angle). Your palm should be facing your body as it lands, as if you are holding a glass of water in your hand. Similar to swinging a baseball bat, turn your body forcefully and let your hand follow through, after your hip and shoulder. Quickly return back to the basic position.

Begin in close range by dipping the knees and the hip.

Use the body torque to create a powerful short hook.

Begin in close range by dipping your knees and hips.

Right Hook

How to: Start close to your opponent; do not attempt to hook from far away. Begin by dipping your left knee slightly and squaring up your hips to the opponent. Transfer your weight to the ball of your lead foot as you start to pivot your hip. Simultaneously bring your elbow up to a horizontal position, parallel to the floor. (Your arm will now be bent at a 90-degree angle.) Your palm should be facing your body as it lands, as if you are holding a glass of water in your hand. Similar to swinging a baseball bat, turn your body forcefully and let the hand follow through after your hip and shoulder. Quickly return back to the basic position.

Lead by turning your hip and shoulder; follow through and return the punch quickly.

DEFENDING AGAINST HOOKS

Cover Up (Block)

On the same side as the oncoming hook, cover the side of your head with your glove. Touch your ear with your glove, look straight ahead at your opponent, and tuck your chin into your shoulder. Make sure to keep your elbow in and down, as close to your body as you can to protect your head and body from the blow.

Lifting your arm will expose your ribs and midsection. This block will protect you from punches and kicks to the head and body from close range.

Deflection into a Grab (Block)

Cover up as described above but instead of just covering your head to block the hook, bring up the point of your elbow and drive it into the fist or arm of your opponent as you simultaneously step in for the grab.

As you block the punch, step in and reach across your body, grabbing the side of your opponent's head with your free hand. Pull his head down to position for a knee strike.

Deflection into a grab.

Covering up to block a hook.

Begin in close range by dipping the knees and the hip.

Quickly lower slightly under the hook.

Bob and Weave (Evasion)

To avoid the hook, you can bob and weave. To execute the bob and weave simply dip the knees a little more and rotate your hips out and back, allowing your head and torso to drop down a little under the punch while still keeping your guard up. Your head and shoulders will travel directly under the hook and to the opposite side, making a "U" shape. Keep the movement small; the wider your evasions the less balance you will maintain, and the less likely you will be able to execute a good counterattack.

Turn the hip and come back up outside the hook at an angle, ready to counterpunch.

STRIKES: UPPERCUTS

Left Uppercut

The uppercut is a powerful close-range power punch. When used as part of a three- or four-punch combination, it can be difficult to see coming, and thus very effective. The uppercut is also effective when thrown while an opponent is covering up.

How to: Begin by bending your knees (in a crouching position), squaring your hips, and keeping your hands up. Drive off the ball of your left foot as you begin to rotate your hips toward your opponent. Drive up explosively from the hips and legs to initiate the uppercut, and then rotate your left hand so that your palm is facing you as you drive it straight up from the shoulder. Return immediately to the basic position.

Bend your knees and keep your hands up.

Explode up from the legs for power.

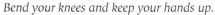

Right Uppercut

How to: Begin by bending your knees (in a crouching position), squaring your hips, and keeping your hands up. Drive off the ball of your right foot as you begin to rotate your hips toward your opponent. Drive up explosively from the hips and legs to initiate the uppercut, and then rotate your right hand so that your palm is facing you as you drive it straight up from the shoulder. Return immediately to the basic position.

Uppercut Tips

- Your hand should move down and then up only about three to four inches.
- Generate power by dipping your body with your legs, not by excessively lowering your punching hand.
- Lead in with a jab or hook and throw the uppercut when you are in close to your opponent. Do not attempt to land from far away.
- The uppercut is especially effective when your opponent's head is down, covering in a defensive position.
- A good follow-up to the uppercut is a hook. Both punches are thrown in close range.
- Remember to keep your opposite hand up to protect your face while executing the punch.

Bend your knees and keep your hands up.

Explode up from the legs for power.

DEFENDING AGAINST UPPERCUTS

Catch (Block)

You will be able to block most uppercuts simply by keeping your hands and forearms in front of your head and body. To catch an uppercut simply turn the palm down a little and catch the uppercut with your glove on the same side.

The taller fighter fades to avoid the uppercut...

Catching the uppercut.

Fade (Evasion)

The fade is executed by moving the shoulders and head straight back to avoid an uppercut. Again you want to miss getting hit by only the smallest possible fraction to enable you to throw a counterpunch.

...and counters with a left hook.

STRIKES: BODY PUNCHES

Jab

Body punching is popular in Western boxing and American kickboxing matches, but is not used often in Muay Thai bouts. This is due to the fact that lowering the head to deliver one of these blows exposes the fighter to an elbow to the head or a knee to the face. When training or fighting using full Thai boxing rules, disregard body-punching techniques, as you can be vulnerable. We will describe the body punches for those who may be training for one of the many fights that outlaw knees and elbows to the head.

How to: Begin by bending at the knees and at the waist. You want your left shoulder even with your target (your opponent's midsection). From here rotate your hips and extend your left (lead) hand and arm fully, keeping the left elbow down and turning the forearm over so that the palm is down and the knuckles land in a level position. Snap the arm forward at the elbow joint, and don't let the elbow come up or out while throwing the jab to the body. Make sure that your chin is tucked in to your shoulder and that your right hand is covering your face, ready to catch an oncoming punch. Return back to the basic standing position as quickly as possible.

> ### Jab Tips
> - Throw the jab from the shoulder with your chin tucked in.
> - Keep your elbow in and down.
> - Snap the punch at the elbow—do not "push" with the punch.
> - Return the punch back to your head as fast as you threw it, coming back to the basic fighting stance.
> - Keep your opposite hand up to protect yourself.
> - Put your shoulder into the punch and create torque at the hips.

Lower your body by bending your knees. Throw a jab to the gut.

Cross Tips

- Bend at the knees and waist. Do not lean forward.
- Relax until the very end when you "snap" the punch.
- Rotate your hips forcefully and pivot on the back foot as you snap at the end of the punch.
- Keep a slight bend in the knees to maintain balance.
- Imagine you are punching through a glass window: As soon as you throw the punch, return the hand to the starting position.

Right Cross

How to: Begin by bending at the knees and at the waist. You want your left shoulder even with your target (your opponent's midsection). From this position quickly rotate your hips and extend your right hand and arm fully, keeping your right elbow down and turning your forearm over so that the palm is down and the knuckles land in a level position. Snap your arm forward at the elbow joint, and don't let the elbow come up or out while throwing the jab. Do not lean forward at the trunk, as this will disrupt your balance, take away power from your punch, and leave you vulnerable for a counter.

Dip the body for a right cross to the gut.

Left Hook

How to: Begin from close range, dipping your knees and bending a little at the waist. Pivot on the ball of your lead (left) foot, then turn your hip to the left, and simultaneously bring the elbow to a horizontal position, parallel to the floor. Your palm should be facing your body as the punch lands, as if you are holding a glass of water in your hand. You want to keep your knees bent a little for balance and power. Similar to swinging a baseball bat, turn your body forcefully and let the hand follow through, after your hip and shoulder, snapping the punch through the last two inches. Quickly return back to the basic position.

Hook Tips

- Turn your body first, then let your hand follow the turn of the body. Do not use the arm to hook.
- Keep your opposite hand held high and maintain visual contact with your opponent.
- Create torque by rotating your hips putting your body mass into the punch.
- Throw the hook hard to the liver when the opponent is covering his face.

Dip your knees and turn your hips to set up the punch.

Turn your body hard and aim the left hook to the liver.

Right Hook

How to: Begin from close range, dipping your knees and bending a little at the waist. Pivot on the ball of your back foot, then turn your hips to the right, and simultaneously bring the elbow to a horizontal position, parallel to the floor. Your palm should be facing your body as the punch lands, as if you are holding a glass of water in your hand. You want to keep your knee bent a little for balance and power. Similar to swinging a baseball bat, turn your body forcefully and let your hand follow through after your hip and shoulder, snapping the punch through the last two inches. Quickly return back to the basic position.

A right hook to the body.

Left Uppercut

How to: Begin by bending your knees deep. While keeping your hands up, bend your left arm, but do not allow it to drop below your waistline. Drive up and rotate explosively from the hips and legs to initiate the uppercut, and then rotate your left hand so that your palm is facing you as you drive it straight up from the shoulder. Return immediately to the basic position. This punch is best landed in close range and after stepping around to the right in a semicircle to get the most power from hip rotation.

1. Hook to the head to lift the opponent's guard.

2. Sidestep around at a 90-degree angle, as shown.

3. Dip your knees and turn your hips to set up the punch.

4. Explode with an uppercut to the solar plexus.

Right Uppercut

How to: Begin by bending the knees deep. While keeping the hands up, bend your right arm but do not allow it to drop below your waistline. Drive up and rotate explosively from the hips and legs to initiate the uppercut and then rotate your right hand so that your palm is facing you as you drive it straight up from the shoulder. Return immediately to the basic position. This punch is best landed in close range and after stepping around to the left in a semicircle to get the most power from hip rotation.

DEFENDING AGAINST BODY PUNCHES

Blocking

All punches to the body are blocked in the same manner, using the elbows and forearms. Simply keeping your arms in close to your body and covering your head with your gloves will guard you from in-close punches. Letting your guard down or raising an arm to block a higher punch will expose your body and leave you vulnerable to a body punch.

Evading

Simply taking one or two short steps around your opponent will take you out of range of any body punches.

Counterattacking

In boxing, keeping your focus on your opponent and looking for openings to deliver counterpunches is the key for fighting in close. With Muay Thai, however, there are fewer attempts at body punching because of the ability to grab (clench), elbow, and knee in addition to body punches. For self-defense purposes the knee and elbow are the most effective choices in a close-range situation.

Keeping your arms close to your body and covering your head with your glove will block most in-close punches.

Dropping low for a body punch can leave you open for an elbow or a knee.

STRIKE: SPINNING BACKFIST

A spinning backfist is an advanced technique delivered with the bottom of the fist. This punch, when used correctly and sparingly, can be effective and powerful. If used incorrectly or too often, it can leave you in serious trouble because of the simple counters and blocks. Also, this is a punch that must be set up correctly. If someone who does not have sufficient experience using it throws it without setting it up, disaster will follow.

How to: Step across your centerline on either side, covering the side of your head with the hand you are not going to punch with. Lift the elbow of the arm you are striking with and lead with the elbow. Completing the initial step should bring one foot well ahead of and across the other, and put the hip in a diagonal position. As you complete your turn, look over your shoulder and eye your target. As you forcefully rotate your hip, let your arm extend as you follow through with the back of your fist and come back to the original position. It is important to set this technique up with a series of punches, or to use it if you are already turning, such as after taking a low round kick.

1. Step across with the jab to set up the backfist.

2. Lead with the elbow as you turn your hips and torso and eye your target.

3. Land the punch with the bottom of your fist.

DEFENDING AGAINST
THE SPINNING BACKFIST

Keep your guard up and block the punch with the forearms or an elbow.

Keep your guard up to block the spinning punch.

STRAIGHT KICKS

Jab Kick

Also known as the foot jab or push kick, this is a basic kick that can be used for both offensive and defensive purposes. This kick is also effective for creating openings, intercepting an attack, setting up combinations, and disrupting an opponent's timing, rhythm, and balance. Targets include the abdomen, solar plexus, groin, and sometimes the chin.

How to: Begin by lifting your lead leg and bending your knee. Turn your base foot outward for balance and quickly bring the knee of your kicking leg up toward your chest. Push your kicking foot straight ahead; the movement of your foot will be a straight line, like a spear shooting forward and piercing the target. Push with the ball of your foot as you explode through the end of the kick. To maintain your balance and return to the basic starting position when using the lead foot to kick with, be sure to practice letting that foot land in front. Do not telegraph the kick by taking any steps forward or moving any other part of your body while kicking.

Pick up the knee to begin the straight lead leg kick.

Push the ball of the foot and explode through the target.

Cross Kick

The cross kick is executed with the back foot and is more powerful but generally has less speed than the kick off the lead leg. This kick is effective for creating openings, intercepting an attack, setting up combinations, and disrupting an opponent's timing, rhythm, and balance. Targets include the abdomen, solar plexus, groin, and on occasion the chin.

How to: Turn your base foot outward for balance and quickly bring the knee of your kicking leg up toward your chest. Push your kicking foot straight ahead; the movement of your foot will be a straight line, like a spear shooting forward and piercing the target. Push with the ball of your foot as you explode through the end of the kick. When using the back foot to kick with, be sure to practice letting that foot land back in its original position to maintain your balance. Do not telegraph the kick by moving any other part of the body while kicking, or taking any steps forward.

Side Kick

The side kick is not often used because in Thai boxing the basic position requires you to be facing ahead instead of sideways. However, you never know where you may end up in a fight and it is good to be able to strike from many possible angles. Assume that you have ended up in a sideways position on either side. The kick is somewhat similar to the jab kick, except the tool for striking in the side kick is the edge of the foot instead of the ball of the foot.

How to: Turn the foot you are standing on so that the toes face sideways at 90 degrees. Bend your kicking leg across your body with the knee going toward your opposite shoulder. Quickly extend the kicking leg and sharply turn the hip into the kick. The blade of the foot will land and the typical target is an exposed midsection.

The cross kick can be used to intercept a straight punch.

An example of a side kick, a beneficial technique that is used occasionally.

DEFENDING AGAINST BASIC KICKS

Inside-Foot Parry (Block)

It is important to practice this drill often, as its timing and execution require time to master. As the jab kick comes forward toward your midsection, step slightly back with the back foot, sweeping your left hand in a semicircular arc downward in order to catch the kicking foot and "sweep it" toward the centerline of your opponent's body. Sweeping the opponent's leg will unbalance him, as his body will turn with his leg as you sweep it. This gives you an opportunity to deliver a quick round kick.

Catch the opponent's foot as he kicks, swing it toward his center...

...and counter with a round kick to the turned leg.

Outside-Foot Parry (Block)

As the jab kick comes forward toward your midsection, take a slight step back with the rear foot, sweeping your right hand in a semicircular arc downward in order to catch the kicking foot, and "sweep it" away from the centerline of your opponent's body. Sweeping the opponent's leg will unbalance him, as his body will turn with his leg as you sweep it outward, giving you an opportunity to deliver a quick punch.

Turn the captured foot away from your opponent's center...

Knee Block (Block)

Block the foot jab by bending your lead knee and using that knee to disrupt the jab kick. Be sure that you keep your hands up and chin down to protect yourself and maintain your balance as you block the kick.

Use the knee to block the straight kick.

Hip Fade (Evasion)

As the kick is heading for your midsection, quickly bend your waist and shoot your hips back to avoid contact and return back to your basic position. This movement can be executed at the last fraction of a second and allows you to stay in close range, which will allow you to deliver a fast counterpunch, grab, or elbow strike.

...and counter with a fast punch.

Use the hip fade to avoid contact.

ROUND KICKS AND SWITCH KICKS

Round Kick

The round kick is a trademark Muay Thai strike. Unlike similar martial arts kicks, the Thai round kick does not involve kicking with the foot, nor is there a "snapping" of the knee joint, but rather there is a complete transfer of the body mass into the kick with full speed and power being transferred through the hip. Thai round kicks can be thrown to the leg, body, or head on either side or used to disrupt an opponent's balance, movement, or become a knockout blow. Use of the round kick to the leg, for example, can create a number of openings for punches and take away an essential skill for every fighter—the ability to stand!

The round kick can be practiced on the long heavy bag, the Thai pads, and in light sparring. The bag practice will allow you to work the mechanics of the kick with full power and is also good to condition and toughen the shins. Begin with the kick low on the bag and just practice turning over the hip; trying to kick high before you learn to turn the kick over will be detrimental. Working the Thai pads will allow you to throw the kick at varying heights and force you to defend against a partner's counterattack. And finally, practice in sparring will allow you to see if you can really hit a moving target and land with the right timing and distance.

The effectiveness of the round kick has been proven not only in the kickboxing ring, but also by the numerous NHB and "Ultimate" fighters learning and using it in the past decade. The kick takes a great deal of practice to learn, but simple physics can describe the basis of its effectiveness:

Mass x Acceleration x Speed = Power

How to: Begin in the basic position, left foot forward for right-handed fighters (switch sides for southpaws), hands up and elbows down. After initiating the kick by turning on the ball of your lead foot, rotate your entire body, transferring all of your body weight to the ball of that foot. Swing your hips and shoulders together and let your kicking leg follow the body around. You want to imagine that you are cutting your target in half with the shin; the kicking leg makes a circle through the target, straightening your kicking leg fully at the end. The torque you create in turning your hip over will create a powerful blow.

Observe a professional baseball player swinging a baseball bat—his body is loose and relaxed. The swing starts at the hip and the entire body is forcefully rotated into the swing. Finally the bat follows through with all the force behind it. Think of your kicking shin as that baseball bat and follow the same movement to create a powerful round kick.

The round kick to the leg uses the torque of your hips to drive the shin through the target.

Swing your body mass around at the hip for a powerful round kick.

Set up the switch kick with a right hand to distract the opponent.

Switch feet at a 45-degree angle and transfer your weight to the ball of your right foot.

Switch Kick

The switch kick follows the same movement as the round kick, except you will throw the kick with your lead leg. Like the round kick, it is very powerful and effective.

How to: Begin in the basic position: left foot forward, hands high, elbows in, weight evenly balanced. Here you initiate the kick by switching feet. You can switch feet by taking a slow deliberate step to the right side (left for southpaws) and a little forward, or you can quickly switch feet replacing one foot with the other and following through immediately with the kick.

After initiating with the step forcefully rotate your entire body, transferring all of your body weight to the ball of the foot you are not kicking with. Swing the hip and shoulder together and let your kicking leg follow the body around. You want to imagine that you are cutting your target in half with the shin; the kicking leg should make a circle through the target, and you should completely straighten the kicking leg at the end of the kick. The torque you create in turning your hip over will create a powerful blow.

Using the power generated by the body, drive the shin through the target. The kick can also be thrown with the lead leg to the opponent's inside thigh. While that blow is not as powerful, it can disrupt the opponent's rhythm and set up a combination.

DEFENDING AGAINST THE ROUND KICK AND SWITCH KICK

Leg Check

To block a low kick and keep your balance, lift up your leg a little and bend at the knee. Your knee should be raised to 10 o'clock or 2 o'clock (depending on which side). Don't bring the leg straight up. Typically, check the leg on the same side as you receive the kick; that is, if the kick comes to your left side, block with the left leg and vice versa. Also, try to block with your knee, as this will hurt your opponent significantly more than it will you. When you check the leg, cover your head with your gloves and your ribs with your elbows. This wall of defense protects you from the kick regardless of its height.

Without switching feet, kick with your lead shin to the inside of the opponent's thigh as he advances forward.

Do not stand square to the opponent when kicking. You want to be at a 45-degree angle as shown here.

Check the kick high on the shinbone at 45 degrees to stop its path.

Catch the Leg

As your opponent throws a round kick at body level, step around to the left or right. If the kick is coming around on your left side, step right; if it is coming to your right side, step to your left. The step takes the power away from the kick. Now simultaneously use your arm to catch the kick on the same side. Sweep the hand around and hold the opponent's foot tightly in the bend of your arm, as close to your body as you can. Be sure to protect your face with your free hand to avoid a straight punch. You now have an opportunity to attack your opponent while he is off balance and in your grip. You may be able to post, which is a term used to describe holding your hand on an opponent's head, hip, or shoulder (with your arm completely straight) to control his movement.

Here are two different options for attacking after you've caught your opponent's leg.

Option 1: Post your free hand in your opponent's face or throat and quickly advance forward, forcing him to balance on one foot. This is known as the *plow*. After a couple of steps, shove him as you release his leg and deliver a quick low kick to the leg the opponent is standing on to send him to the ground.

Step off and catch the opponent's leg while posting his face or shoulder.

Take two quick steps with the lead foot to throw the opponent off balance.

Option 2: Reach across your opponent's body and grab the top of his head, pulling his head down and striking his body or face with a knee strike or an elbow. As you now have control of his head and he is on one leg, step around in a semicircle with your back leg, turn your hip and throw the opponent around and down to the ground.

Shove the opponent and release his leg as you switch feet.

Grab the back of your opponent's head.

Deliver an inside kick to his supporting leg.

Deliver a knee to the face.

Countering the Leg Catch: The Wizzer

To get free and keep from being thrown, slide one hand around the arm that your opponent is using to hold your leg. Next post your other hand into the opponent's head with your elbow locked out completely. Now bend your leg and powerfully drive your knee down to the ground while swinging your body around. This move will bring the opponent down to the ground as shown.

3. Turn forcefully around to the outside of your opponent's center and slide the trapped knee toward the floor.

1. The opponent catches your kick.

2. Bend your knee and underhook the opponent's arm on the same side, posting his head with your straight arm on the opposite side.

4. The result is an opponent in a defenseless position.

After catching a kick, an inexperienced fighter may not post with the free hand. If this is the case, first jerk your leg back toward your body, then deliver a powerful straight punch to the face.

The result of not posting after catching a kick!

Elbow/Arm Block
Keep your elbows in close to your body and hands up to shield you from the body-level kick.

Keep your guard up and elbows close to the body.

Shield and Parry

If the kick is coming toward your head, turn your upper body slightly into the kick, and use both your forearms to receive the kick. Next parry the leg by sweeping it in the same path that it is going, and step slightly back at the same time to allow room for the leg to swing down. For example, if the kick is coming from the left side use your double forearm shield, and use your right hand to sweep the leg along to the right side. Sweep the leg to the left side if it is coming from the right, as this is where the momentum of the kick is going. Your opponent will be off balance and a bit sideways if you parry the leg successfully, and you will be in a good position to throw a counterkick to the leg.

Use the forearms to block the high kick and grab your opponent's shin with the appropriate hand.

Parry the kick in its intended direction.

Parrying the kick turns the opponent off balance and sideways.

ADVANCED KICKS

Cut Kick

This is a sophisticated move that can be devastating if executed correctly and with appropriate timing. As your opponent steps to set up a high kick to your head, step in the same direction as he is (mirror his step). After he has committed to the kick but before it makes contact with you, quickly deliver a low kick to opponent's supporting leg. Your kick should "cut" the leg out from under your opponent. Achieve this by placing your kick at or below the knee.

The cut kick can be done from either side. Should the kick be coming to your left leg, execute the cut kick with the left leg and vice versa.

Cut kick the base leg while the opponent tries a high round kick.

Intercept the Kick

As the opponent steps in closer to set up the round kick, place a jab kick straight to the body or hip quickly and powerfully, before the opponent can land his kick. This will disrupt the kick, push the opponent back, and make him more timid about throwing the kick.

The round kick can also be interrupted by a straight punch to the face, as many fighters let their arms sway out and away from the face when throwing the kick.

Intercept the round kick with a foot jab.

A right hand intercepts the kick!

Spinning Back Kick

This can be a dangerous kick to attempt and only experienced individuals should use it, but learning it offers a good challenge. It can be delivered with a great deal of power if done correctly and can be useful in a fight.

How to: Begin by throwing a left hook to hide the kick and cause your opponent to react by bringing up his hands. As you throw the hook, step over with the lead foot, across your body in a semicircle. Now turn your body quickly so your back is to the opponent (or training bag), look over your shoulder, and eye your target. Now, rotating your hips, drive your right leg straight up with the heel as the kicking tool. With practice you will be able to throw this kick with speed and power. To land this kick you must use timing and throw it when the opponent advances toward you; this is the time to side-step and deliver this kick to the midsection.

Turn backward and eye your opponent.

Distract the opponent with a hook and step over with it.

As you turn your hip, forcefully bring the heel of your foot into the opponent's liver. Return to the basic position.

KNEE STRIKES

Straight Knee

Knee strikes can be used from a standing position or while clenching, are extremely effective close-range weapons, and are simple to learn.

How to: Begin by taking a quick, short step forward with the lead foot, keeping your hands posted in front of your face with palms out toward the opponent to ward off a punch, an elbow, or in order to grab the opponent's head. At the same time let your back knee come upward while you lean your torso back somewhat. Last, drive the knee forward like a spear into the opponent, pushing your hip forward.

The straight knee executed from a clench.

Drive the hip forward for the straight knee.

Targets for the straight knee can be the ribs, solar plexus, or abdomen. You can also make a small jump with your lead foot to deliver more forward force. This is known as a flying knee.

If you are engaged in a clench, the top of the opponent's head should be pulled down and the knees delivered into the body, head, and face.

If you have an opponent clenched you can alternate knees, striking with both in rapid succession. To begin with the right knee, bring the right leg back to make room for the knee, strike, then set the right foot straight down. Bring the left foot back and quickly strike with the left knee, and so on. Keep the opponent in close when not striking and control the range by quickly making room for the knee and then keeping your opponent in close and tight to keep him from having room to counterstrike you.

Round Knee

This is performed just like the round kick, except that instead of driving the shin into the target, you will drive in the knee. This knee is performed in closer range than the kick, but has similar power.

How to: Make a semicircular step and forcefully rotate your hip so that the bent leg swings around and drives into the target. Transfer all of your body weight to the ball of the foot that you are standing on, and pivot on that foot. Your hip and shoulder should rotate at the same time to get your body mass into the knee. This strike is best used when engaged in a clench, but does not have to be.

Make room for the knee by bringing your hip back and straightening your leg.

Make room for the round knee.

Quickly explode through with your knee as you pull the opponent back toward you.

Drive the point of the knee into the target.

Circle Knee

While engaged in the clench, you may find that an opponent's side is exposed. This is an opening for the circle knee.

How to: Bend your leg at the knee and lift it so that the top of your thigh is parallel to the floor. Pivoting on your opposite foot, swing the leg out and away from your opponent's exposed side to create room and generate momentum. Next, using hip rotation, drive the inside tip of your knee in a circular motion into your opponent's exposed side. The knee will only have power if there is sufficient space created between you and the opponent.

Swing the hip out to begin the circle knee.

Lift the opponent's arm from the clench.

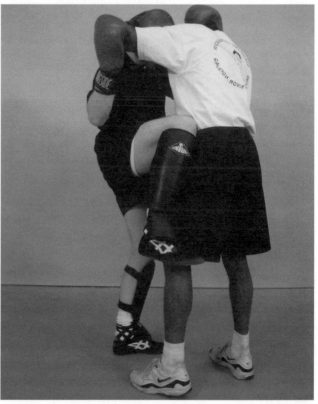

Drive the inside of the knee into the target.

ELBOW STRIKES

The elbow is a dangerous close-range technique that is a specialty of Thai boxing. The elbow is best used after a punch and after getting close to an opponent with a few short steps. It is not advisable for beginners to actually spar with the elbow. Instead, sparring drills with the elbow strikes should be done to learn the necessary control.

Hooking Elbow

When using the hooking elbow, the arms can be extended straight out from the face in a defensive position, or in closer to the face a little above eye level. On either side rotate the wrist across the body, turning over the shoulder and letting the arm bend at the elbow. Sharply drive the point of the elbow into the target (chin, temple, eye, or nose) and quickly return back to the basic position.

You want the elbow to strike quickly and sharply. As with the punch you will not want to "push forward" but instead whip the elbow around, similar to throwing a hook.

Upward Elbow

Keep your arms in close and your hands held high (at or above eye level). Move your arm straight back as though you were patting yourself on the back while covering your face with the opposite hand. The elbow should quickly whip upwards, under the chin of your opponent, similar to an uppercut. This elbow can be done in close-range fighting or as a surprise when engaged in a clench.

The beginning of a hooking elbow from a clench.

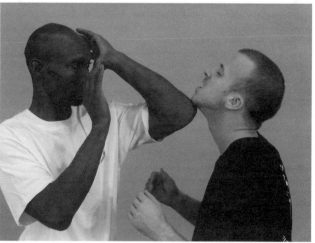

The upward elbow can be a devastating surprise maneuver.

Strike with the point of the elbow by rolling the wrist.

Downward Elbow

If you have negotiated your opponent's face toward the floor and he is bent forward, you can deliver a downward elbow to the back of his head.

How to: Holding the opponent's head down while he is bent forward, raise your opposite hand straight up, and then quickly drive the point of the elbow down onto the base of his head.

Diagonal Elbow

This elbow strike is to be delivered at an angle so as to break through the opponent's guard.

How to: With hands high, at or above eye level, raise the striking arm by lifting the hand straight up in the air. Quickly flip the wrist so that as the elbow travels toward the target in a diagonal line the elbow turns over, coming down between the opponent's hands.

The diagonal elbow flies down at an angle to go through the opponent's guard.

Raise the arm to initiate the downward elbow to the skull.

Inset: Bring the arm down, crashing the tip of the elbow into the target.

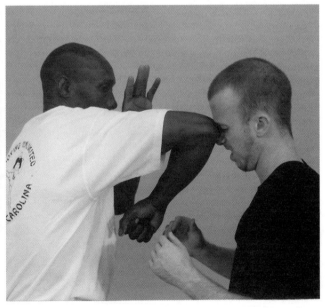

Diagonal elbow finish.

Spinning Elbow

How to: While in close range, step across with your lead foot and forcefully turn your body around, driving the point of your elbow into the opponent's face.

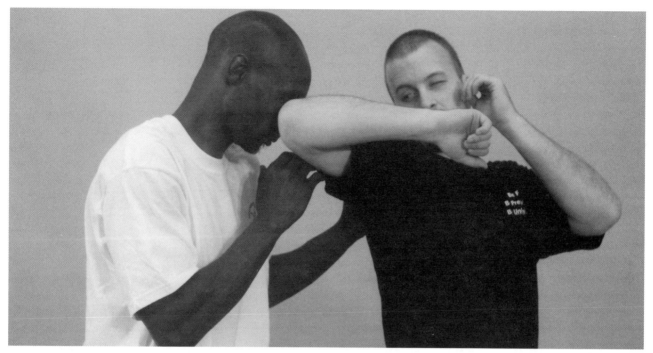

The spinning elbow is an advanced move that can surprise a tired opponent.

BLOCKING THE ELBOW

Use the forearms to block the elbow strikes when fighting in close.

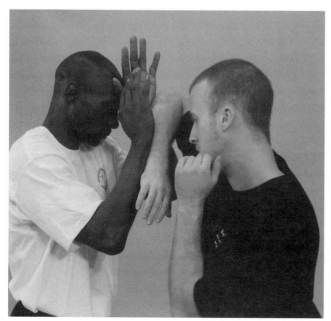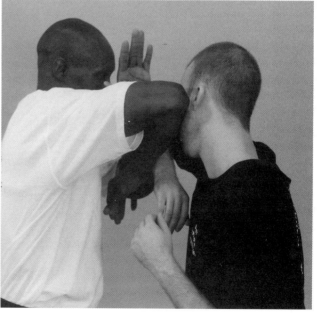

The elbow is blocked using both forearms.   *After blocking, counter with an elbow of your own.*

STRIKES AND DEFENSES

CLENCHING EXERCISES

Clenching (also known as the plum) is a way of controlling and off-balancing an opponent, as well as creating openings for the elbow and knee. The *inside clench* is when you have both hands clasped around the back of the head or neck of your opponent (cross one hand over the other—never interlock your fingers). Get the clench position by shooting in only one arm at a time, grasping the top of the back of your opponent's head while keeping the other elbow up and in front of the face for protection from attack. If you have grasped the head successfully, then quickly follow up with the other hand to complete the clench.

Chad Boykin (left) and NHB competitor Neal Weaver square off.

Shoot the lead hand in and grab the back of the opponent's head.

Wrap the other hand around the head to complete the top clench.

An important exercise to practice often involves having a training partner attack you with aggressive punch combinations while you try to block the punches and clench him. If you get in trouble against an opponent who is throwing good punch combinations, it is important to be able to clench him without losing your composure (dropping your hands or lifting your chin). You clench up this way when you have decided that the opponent is a better puncher than you and you are not winning the exchange.

1. Block the opponent's jab with a brush.

2. Block the opponent's cross with a brush and drive the opposite elbow forward.

3. Use the elbow to block the hook and grab across the attacker's head.

4. Pull him into a knee to lower his head.

5. Finish with a guillotine choke.

The *low clench* looks like a "bear hug" position and is used to apply pressure to an opponent's lower/middle back and neutralize the advantage that he has when his hands are clasped behind your head. Drive a shoulder into your opponent's chest while pulling his lower back with your arms as shown.

To escape low clenches, place your elbows deep into your opponent's collarbones. Next, in one hard motion, explode the hips out and backward and simultaneously thrust the elbows up (into collarbones) and pull the top of opponent's head in.

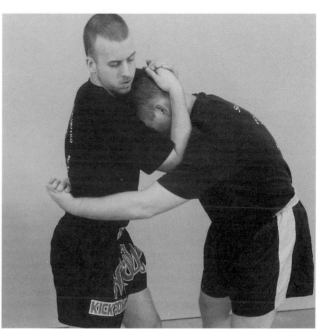

Pull down on the top of the opponent's head and drive your elbows up as you explode back with the hips to break the low clench.

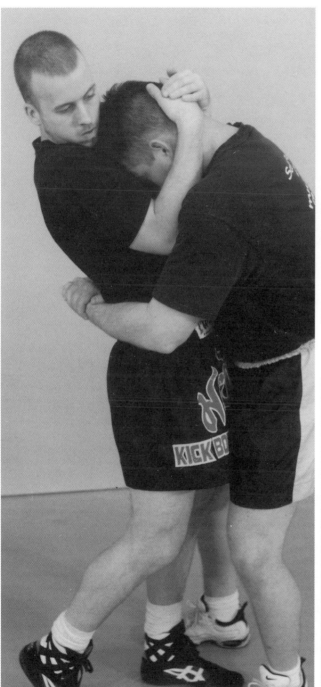

The low clench.

Pull the opponent off balance by jerking his head.

MUAY THAI KICKBOXING

Pivot around as you straighten your arms, locking his head down.

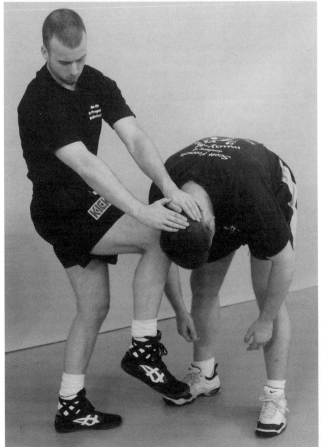

Finish with a knee to the face.

Another simple maneuver to counter this grip is to put your hands under the opponent's chin and push away.

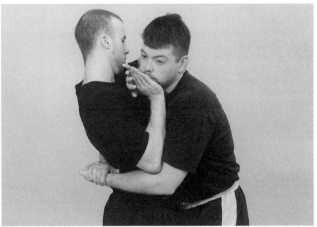

Put your palms under the attacker's chin.

Push his face away to break his low clench.

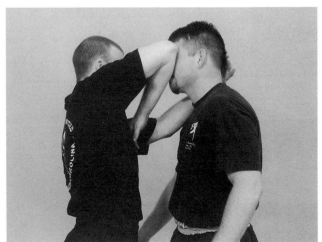

Grip the back of his head and finish with an elbow to the face.

The *spin* is a method of off-balancing and irritating your opponent. From any of the clench positions step around either forward or backward going either to the right or left to swing your hip around and jerk your opponent's head down and in that direction. This can be used to set up a finishing knee, elbow, headbutt, punch, or kick. Holding onto the partner's elbows and taking him in the same direction with the spin will reverse it.

Kickboxer Gene Wright prepares for a spin.

Stepping in a semicircle he jerks his opponent down in the same direction …

... taking him off balance

To reverse this spin, hold on to the opponent's arms.

To take him off balance, jerk him with the momentum he created and make room for an escape or strike.

To escape from the inside position of the clench you can elbow shove by popping one of the opponent's elbows up with your opposite hand, creating an opening to slide the same side hand through.

After shoving the elbow, you can duck under the opponent's arm and move around so that your chest is on the opponent's shoulder, for a choke. Once you have this side shoulder position, slide your inside arm upward and along the throat of your opponent. To apply the choke, bend that arm and squeeze the biceps, allowing no space between your biceps, elbow, and your opponent's throat.

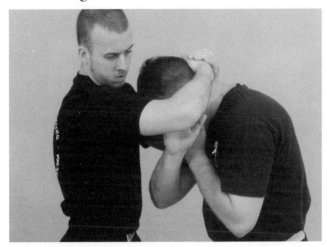

Make room by shoving one of the opponent's elbows.

Slide your opposite arm through the hole you just created.

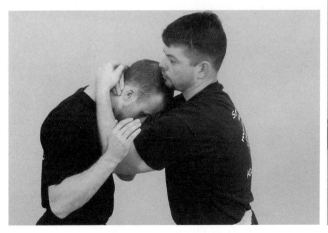

Complete the clench takeover by sliding your other hand through.

Shove the elbow and lift the opponent's arm.

Duck your head under his arm and get a side shoulder position.

A taller person can turn into the choke and wrap the lifted arm around and under the attacker's throat. Turn the hold into a guillotine choke as shown.

Squeeze with the biceps to choke.

To escape the side shoulder choke, a taller fighter can turn into the hold and turn the opponent's head down into a guillotine choke.

The snake is another way to escape from a strong clench. Go over one of his elbows with your arm, placing the point of your elbow into his shoulder joint. Next, place your opposite hand underneath his elbow, bringing your palms together. Crank your outside arm up and use your inside arm to grind your elbow into his shoulder. Your other arm is now lifting the opponent's "free" arm and the torque will create an opening to slide the arm in for the clench.

Grind the point of the elbow into the opponent's shoulder.

Turn the torso to create leverage.

Shoot the other hand inside the hole.

Wrap up the opponent's head to reverse the clench.

64

MUAY THAI KICKBOXING

Some fighters may try to post the hip by placing their hands on the outside of your hips with locked arms, preventing a knee strike. Although this will block a straight knee strike, it is hardly worth the disastrous consequences. Should someone post your hips, simply take some short sharp steps backward and jerk his head down to place a knee to the face.

Or position the opponent's head over his lead leg (so that most of his body weight is on that leg) and drive in a hard leg kick.

The opponent posts your hips to prevent a knee.

Step back and jerk his head down.

Straighten your arms and put your weight on his head.

Finish the exchange with a knee to the face.

If your opponent posts your hips, you can also position his head over either leg.

Now that his weight is on that leg, explode with a round kick to that leg from close range.

To block straight knee strikes, hold on to the inside of your opponent's elbows from the outside of his arms (like with the spin reversal).

Then drive the point of your elbow into his thigh to stop his knee strikes.

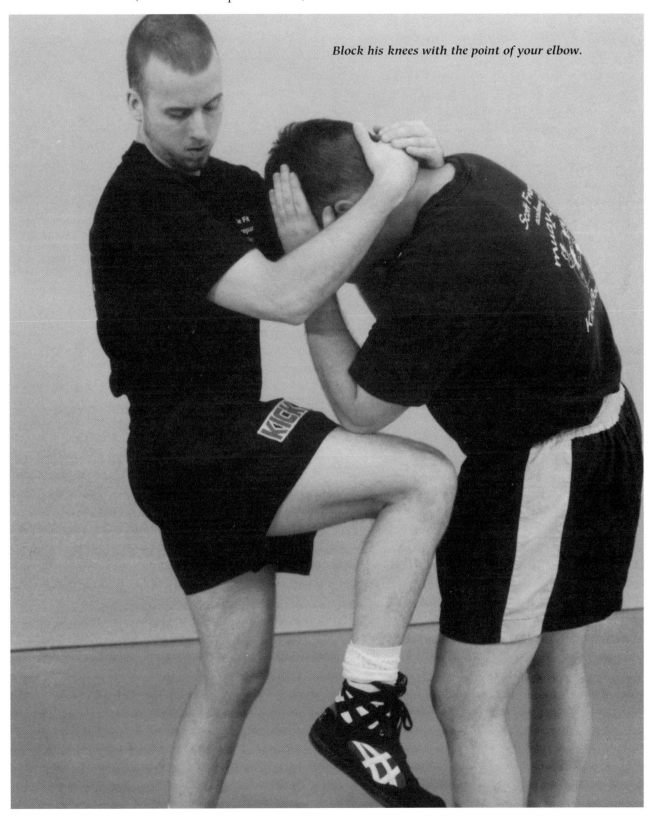

Block his knees with the point of your elbow.

A throw can be done when an opponent attempts a knee strike from the clench. When you feel the opponent make the room necessary to throw the knee, grab the knee as shown. Take the opponent off balance away from the base leg as shown.

Neal Weaver protects his face from the anticipated knee.

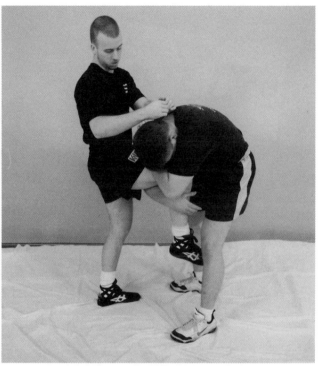

He captures the leg, blocking with the right arm and trapping the leg with the left.

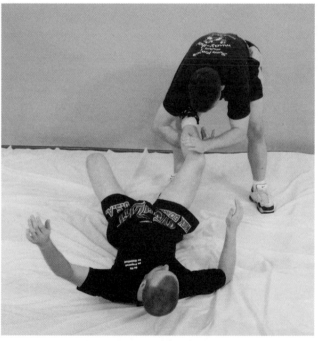

He executes a throw by turning his assailant away from his base leg.

A hip throw is not a legal maneuver in Muay Thai. But it is an effective move in standing confrontations with an opponent facing you or at your side. As your opponent grabs or clenches you, either underhook his arm or hook over his head (as shown). Simultaneously step in between his feet with your foot on the same side as your underhooked arm. Now take a slight step turning both feet straight ahead and position your butt underneath his pelvis by bending at the knees. Now you have *loaded* (positioned him for) the hip throw. To throw the opponent, straighten your legs and lift your butt straight up (your opponent's feet will now be off the ground) and drive the arm you have wrapped around him down and across your body from the shoulder as you turn your hip over in the same direction.

Loading the hip: Throw hips in close with your back bent.

Using leverage, turn the opponent over your hip and to the ground.

COMBINATION STRIKING

It is important to learn to attack with combinations—do not look for one lethal blow or knockout punch. Attacking with combinations will make your opponent have a hard time recovering and counterpunching.

For example, throw two to four punches in succession followed by a low kick or two kicks followed by a couple of punches. The idea is to set up your opponent for your next move like a game of human chess.

Kick low to weaken the opponent's legs and force him to lower his hands, then go high with punches. Punch high at the opponent's face to raise his guard (make him cover up) and then attack his body with a liver punch (left hook to the body) or his legs with a powerful low kick. It is the punch or kick that you do not see coming that is often the knockout blow.

It takes time and practice to learn to think a couple of moves ahead, but it can be done. When punching in combination, use the torque created by the turning of your hips on the punch you threw last to get power for the next blow. In the beginning you should practice punching and kicking off opposite sides left to right and right to left. With experience you will be able to throw off the same side with speed and power (hooking off the jab for example) as well as switching sides.

Remember to be aware of your defense when attacking in combination. Commit to your strikes but keep your guard up. When throwing multiple punches, keep your opposite hand up and bring your punches back fast.

The next chapter describes several combinations that can be practiced in training or sparring. Find the combinations that suit your particular style and strengths, train them regularly, and you will be attacking with combinations without thinking about it.

Training 3 Drills

Sports do not build character. They reveal it.
—Heywood Brown, 1888-1939

Your results and performance are a direct result of how hard you are willing to push yourself in the gym. The will to win is common, but it is the will to *prepare* to win that is most important. Muay Thai training utilizes various pieces of specialized equipment to enhance the fighter's power, speed, technique, reflexes, precision, balance, and timing.

EQUIPMENT

Aside from regular sparring, the nuts and bolts of Thai-boxing training and conditioning is done by experienced coaches using Thai pads, belly pads, and punch mitts. Other important tools include heavy bags, medicine balls, big pads, punch shields, double-end bags, and speed bags. Used correctly, the training equipment can sharpen skills, provide great physical conditioning, and test your inner toughness.

Thai Pads
Thai pads are thick pads held to the forearms with straps and hook and loop closures or steel buckles. They are used to drill combination kicks, knees, elbows, and punches. These pads allow for full-power knee strikes while working the clench positions. Full-power strikes are thrown on a moving target that can hit back!

A good pad holder can train you so that your strikes are fast and powerful. If you hit too slowly, the pad holder can move out of the way or respond with a strike of his own. A good pad trainer stays on his toes and moves as an opponent, reacting with strikes and helping increase the reaction time, skill, and power of his fighter.

Holding the pads correctly means the difference between a productive workout session and one that results in an injury. For example, if an inexperienced pad holder misjudges the range of a strike thrown with full force, the fighter could easily pull muscles. The secret to pad work is practice and a mastery of appropriate range, distance, timing, and keeping constant physical and psychological pressure on your partner. Putting your body weight behind the pads is important; you must provide resistance for each kick. Pictured are correct ways to hold the Thai pads for punches, kicks, and knees.

Stack one pad on top of the other for straight kicks or knees.

Hold the Thai pads at 45 degrees and close to your body for the round kick. The pads should be vertical and you should take the kick low on the forearms, near the elbows.

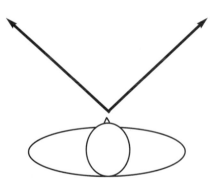

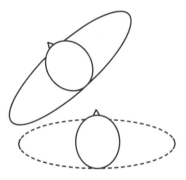

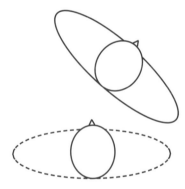

Figure 3A. *The Thai-pad holder must position the pads in a 45-degree angle for the round kick and switch kick, assuming he is squared up with the fighter. If you step before throwing either kick, you must step at this 45-degree angle.*

Figure 3B. *Here is the turn of the body from an overhead view when throwing the round kick.*

Figure 3C. *Here is the turn of the body from an overhead view when throwing the switch kick.*

MUAY THAI KICKBOXING

Hold the pad vertically for the jab at straight arm's length.

Hold the pad at an angle for the uppercut.

The trainer sets up for a right cross.

The blow is parried and countered with a knee.

Belly Pad

The belly pad is a thick pad that straps around the shoulders and waist, protecting the trainer from blows to the abdomen and ribs. Used in combination with the Thai pads, the belly pad allows the fighter to deliver fast, powerful straight kicks and knees to the body while working the Thai pads or punch mitts for punches and round kicks. The belly pad is also used in boxing for work on body punches.

The trainer attacks with a straight punch while the fighter keeps his guard up and delivers a foot jab.

The fighter intercepts a round kick with a foot jab to the belly pad.

The trainer attacks with a straight punch as the fighter slips outside.

The fighter delivers a liver punch to the belly pad.

Big Pad

The big pad is used like a body shield and is essential for training frontal attacks. Use the big pad to drill straight kicks, knees, and body punches. The pad holder should be the aggressor. For example, when in range throw straight kicks and knees as the pad holder advances. Practice body-punch combinations, or clench up and work the knee strikes. The big pad is also good for training in side kicks and spinning back kicks, and can be held sideways for round and switch kicks.

Keep the pad close to your body and put your weight into it for training power kicks and knees.

Punch Shield

This circular pad has handles on opposing sides and is used for body punches and uppercuts, or can be held on the side of your leg to teach the circular motion of a proper leg kick. When working the kick, hold the shield on the side of the leg so that your partner trains to hit the correct part of the leg. Also, make sure to keep your knee bent to avoid knee damage while using this pad for kicks. While training the leg kick, it is a good idea to use your free hand to simulate punches with a blocker so that your fighter can work on landing the kick while fending off an attack.

The trainer simulates a straight punch as the fighter brushes it away.

He counters with a strong leg kick.

The trainer simulates a hook as the fighter covers up.

The fighter counters with a powerful low kick.

Punch/Focus Mitts

These small, hand-sized mitts are used to teach proper punches, range, and defense. Focus mitts allow you to simulate a fight by pressuring your partner and allowing you to throw punches back at him, which teaches defense and counterpunching. As with the Thai pads, experience can make all the difference.

It is important to train your partner on the pads as though you were sparring. Do not simply stand still and practice punches, but rather move around and make the fighter judge the range constantly while throwing kicks and punches of your own so that they must be defensive as well as offensive in training.

The following is a pad drill that includes both defense and offense.

The pad holder squares up.

The pad holder throws a jab as the fighter slips.

The pad holder keeps the pad at arm's length for the straight right hand.

He meets the left hook close and at centerline.

Heavy Bag

The heavy bag is used to develop power in your kicks and punches. The Thai-style bag is six feet long and allows for leg kicks as well as punches. The boxer's punching bag is usually four feet long and is used exclusively for punches. Train on the bag so that you can throw with full speed and power for the duration of the round without rest. Work the bag as if it were a real opponent; move your head as if you were slipping punches; circle around and practice your footwork; and find the right distance from the bag to get full power on your punches and kicks.

Work the heavy bag at various angles. Concentrate on angles, technique, and power to develop skills and stamina.

MUAY THAI KICKBOXING

Double-End Bag

This small bag is anchored at the top and bottom end and is used to develop quick punches, hand-eye coordination, accuracy, defense, and timing. Because this bag springs back at you every time you land a punch, it is a great tool for teaching defense, reaction time, and evasions. When you're further from the bag, work the jab and cross, then get close and work the straight as well as hooking and uppercut punches, all while dodging and keeping your hands up.

The double-end bag is practical for developing head movement, speed, hand-eye coordination, and defensive reflexes.

Speed Bag

Many boxing gyms provide small speed bags. These bags are good for developing rhythm and hand-eye coordination, as well as gaining muscular endurance in the shoulders. Keep the hands up, elbows out, and lightly hit the bag in a circular motion in the same spot. Try to dictate the pace during the round. This exercise is like jumping rope for the hands.

Medicine Ball

The medicine ball is a leather ball that can weigh from 5 to 15 pounds. This great tool can be used to toughen the abdominals, provide resistance in plyometric exercises (throwing and passing), and used in punching drills. Exercises with the medicine ball are featured later in this book.

Timer

Electric timers are a valuable tool for keeping track of rounds (2 to 4 minutes) and rest periods (15 to 60 seconds). Timers are also available that will sound at pre-set intervals (15 to 45 seconds) for advanced interval conditioning.

SPARRING

Sparring is the only real way to test your skills. You can develop tremendous power training on the pads, but power only matters if you can land your strikes on an opponent. There are three levels of sparring that relate to the force of the contact.

Touch sparring is sparring at full speed, but with as little power as possible. The goal is to touch your sparring partner with your strikes at about 20 percent of your full power. Touch sparring allows you to test your skills and speed without fear of serious pain (there will be plenty of that down the road if you want). You have to crawl before you walk, and walk before you can run. It is best to spar this way with more experienced fighters, as they have more control than a less-experienced person.

Medium-contact sparring should be done at 50 to 60 percent of your full power. Most productive sparring happens at this level. Here you will find out what you need to work on and develop your own style.

If you are preparing for a fight, however, you should spar with more power and get used to the intensity and pressure. This is *hard sparring* and it is 75+ percent of your full power. You want to spar with opponents that are better than you—this is the only way to improve. Make sure that you trust this person to help you develop though; you don't want to just get your ass kicked all the time for nothing.

Sparring should be beneficial to everyone. Less-experienced boxers will improve, thus giving better competition for the more advanced athletes. Likewise, as you progress, you can give a little back and work with some new folks to help them along. Unfortunately, sparring between two undisciplined, inexperienced boxers can become a pissing contest where no one wins. Practicing the following drills will let you get used to blocking and countering various attacks. With regular practice at these drills you will gain the confidence to begin sparring.

FOOTWORK DRILLS

Square Drill

Begin in basic position: left foot forward, hips straight ahead, hands up, elbows in. Move two steps forward, stepping short with the left foot and sliding the right foot, ending up back in the basic position. Next, step to the left with the left foot and slide the right to cover the distance; go two steps. Going backward, step back with the right foot and slide the left foot to cover the distance; go two steps in this direction, also. Finally, step to the right with the right foot and again slide the left to come back to the basic position. Now you have completed a square going two steps in each of the four directions. Simply remember to step with the foot of the direction that you want to go (back foot going backward, left foot going left, etc.).

To add to the footwork drill, add punch combinations to the footwork, beginning with the jab (1) with each step, and the cross (2)

while sliding the opposite foot. This teaches you to jab going in any direction and coordinate hand and foot movement. Add any fluid punch combination after the steps have been completed. For example, step and drag with the 1-2, then add the 3-6-3 while still. Or to work the basic punches, add one punch each step (1, 1-2, 1-2-3).

Figure 3D shows the proper way to step to maintain balance. Each *solid arrow* indicates that that foot steps in the indicated direction; the *broken arrow* indicates that that foot slides the same distance. The figures on the left illustrate moving forward and backward (from top to bottom). The figures on the right illustrate moving left and right (from top to bottom).

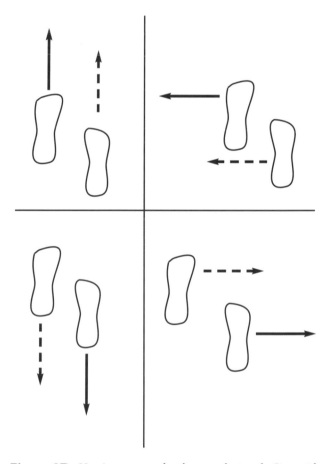

Figure 3D. *Here's an example of proper footwork. Step with the foot that has a solid line, while sliding the foot with the broken line. Sidestep and punch the charging opponent instead of backing up. This puts you in a good position and takes away the steam of his attack.*

ROPE DRILL

Tie a rope across a 15- to 20-foot area just below head level. Begin at one end of the rope and move forward practicing proper footwork, taking short steps with the lead foot and sliding the back foot. After you have taken each step, bob and weave (see Chapter 2) under the rope on each side. You want your head to drop slightly below the rope, just as if it were a punch. Continue until you are at the end of the rope, then pivot and repeat for a three-minute round.

Once you have mastered the above drill you can add punch combinations after you bob and weave following each step toward the end of the rope. For example, step and drag, bob and weave right and left, then throw a right cross-left hook-right cross (2-3-2).

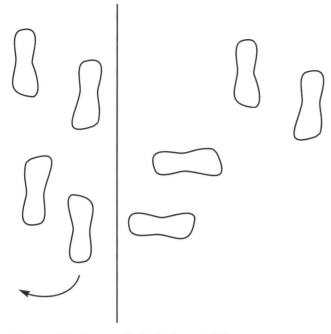

Figure 3E. *Pivot on the ball of your left foot, swinging your back foot in an arc. This is essential for dealing with a charging opponent.*

KICKS AND KNEES

Have a trainer hold the big pad. Begin with 20 jump squats, then move your partner back with the straight kick. Each time you move him back, you advance one step until you have moved the length of the floor. Finish with 10 skip knees (combination knees) and work your way back down the floor for five minutes. Finish off the round with 20 jump squats. This drill develops powerful kicks and knees as well as endurance and leg strength.

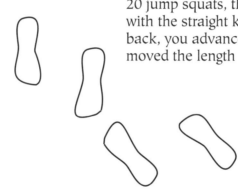

Figure 3F. *This illustrates stepping to the right (outside the opponent's jab) and then turning so that your opponent is sideways.*

DRILL KEY

The following key will be used in the drills to keep the instructions concise. For example, the shorthand 2-3-2 would describe a right cross-left hook-right cross combination. Note: when the text reads, "From," as in, "From the 1-2," that indicates that you are defending against an opponent who's just thrown that combination.

Strikes:
1 = jab
2 = right cross
3 = left hook
4 = right hook
5 = left uppercut
6 = right uppercut
7 = jab to the body
8 = right cross to the body
9 = left hook to the body
10 = right hook to the body
11 = left uppercut to the body
12 = right uppercut to the body
13 = spinning backfist

Elbows:
Elbow = E
Right hooking elbow = RHE
Left hooking elbow = LHE
Right diagonal elbow = RDE
Left diagonal elbow = LDE
Upward elbow = UE
Hooking elbow = HE

Kicks:
Round kick = RK
Switch kick = SWK
Cross kick = CK
Jab kick = JK

Knees:
Knee = N
Circle knee = CN
Straight knee = SN
Skip knees = SKN

Other Moves:
Bob and weave = BW
Grab = G
Clench = C
Spin = SP

THAI PAD DRILLS

Beginner Level
- Jab-round kick (1-RK)
- Cross kick-jab (CK-1)
- Jab kick-cross (JK-2)
- Cross-switch kick (2-SWK)
- Jab-jab-cross (1-1-2)
- Jab-cross-left hook (1-2-3)
- Jab-cross-left hook-round kick (1-2-3-RK)
- Jab-left hook (1-3)
- Round kick-cross-left hook (RK-2-3)
- Jab-right hooking elbow (1-RHE)
- Cross-left hooking elbow (2-LHE)
- Jab-cross-left hook-right diagonal elbow (1-2-3-RDE)
- Cross-left hook-cross-left hook to the body (2-3-2-9)
- Left hook-cross-left hook (3-2-3)
- Cross-left hook-cross-switch kick (2-3-2-SWK)
- Left hook-cross-left hook-round kick (3-2-3-RK)
- Jab kick or cross kick-straight knee (JK or CK-SN)
- Jab kick-cross-hook-cross (JK-2-3-2)
- Upward elbow-hooking elbow-grab-straight knee (UE-HE-G-SN)
- Clench-skip knees-spin (C-SKN-SP)
- Jab-inside kick to the lead leg-cross-round kick (1-inside kick to lead leg-2-RK)

Pictured is the jab-cross-hook-round kick drill on the Thai pads (1-2-3-RK). Continued on following page

COUNTERSTRIKING PAD COMBINATIONS

- Brush the jab: Jab-jab-cross (1-1-2)
- Slip the jab: Cross-hook-cross-switch kick (2-3-2-SWK)
- Brush the jab: Brush the cross-cross-hook-cross (2-3-2)
- Brush the jab: Jab-cross-hook-round kick (1-2-3-RK)
- Body block the right hook: Cross-hook-cross-switch kick (2-3-2-SWK)
- Body block the left hook: Hook-cross-hook-switch kick (3-2-3-SWK)
- Fade the hips to dodge the jab or cross kick: Round kick or switch kick (RK or SWK)
- Fade the hips to dodge the jab or cross kick: Cross-hook-grab-knee (2-3-G-N)
- Thai brush the jab or cross: Hooking elbow (HE)
- Leg check the round kick or switch kick: Cross-switch kick (2-SWK)
- Thai brush the jab or cross: Elbow-clench-skip knee (E-C-SKN)
- Slip-slip (from the 1-2): Left hook-cross-left hook-round kick (3-2-3-RK)
- Slip-bob and weave: Bob and weave (from the 1-2-3)-cross-switch kick (BW-2-SWK)
- Leg check: Switch kick-cross-hook-cross (SWK-2-3-2)
- Leg check-brush-slip-bob and weave (from RK-1-2-3): Cross-hook-cross-switch kick (2-3-2-SWK)
- Body block: Grab-knee-clench-skip knee-spin (G-N-C-SKN-SP)

The slip-cover-hooking elbow combination (slip-cover-HE).

      MUAY THAI KICKBOXING

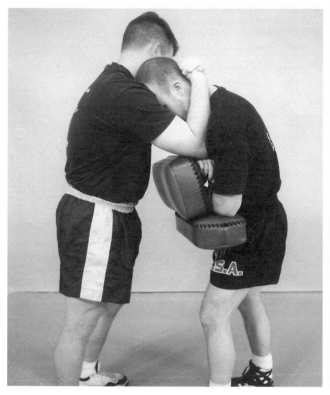

Here is the correct way to strike with skip knees. From the clench, keep the hips close to control the opponent until you are ready to knee.

Bring your leg back and explode through with a straight knee, pushing the hip forward at the end.

Set that foot straight down and bring the opposite leg back.

Deliver that knee the same way.

THAI PAD DRILLS

Intermediate Level
- Jab-cross-left uppercut-cross-left hook (1-2-5-2-3)
- Cross kick-left hook-cross-switch kick (CK-3-2-SWK)
- Jab kick-cross-hook-cross-grab-knee (JK-2-3-2-G-N)
- Cross-switch kick-clench-skip knee-circle knee-spin (2-SWK-C-SKN-CN-SP)
- Jab-jab-cross-uppercut-cross-switch kick (1-1-2-5-2-SWK)
- Uppercut-hook-uppercut-clench-skip knees (6-3-6-C-SKN)
- Jab-cross-left hook-round kick-grab-knee (1-2-3-RK-G-N)
- Jab-cross kick-knee-grab-elbow (1-CK-N-G-E)
- Round kick (step back)-cross-left hook (RK-2-3)
- Jab-cross-hook-cross-hook-elbow (1-2-3-2-3-E)

SPARRING DRILLS

Sparring drills should focus on positioning, range manipulation, balance, timing, distance, footwork, rhythm, and eye contact.

- Brush partner's jab-return the jab.
- Body block the hook off both sides-return the hook.
- Throw and block the 1-low RK (leg check, same side).
- Throw and block the 1-mid RK (body block).
- Throw and block the 1-high RK (double shield).
- Throw and block the 2-low SWK (leg check, same side).
- Throw and block the 2-middle SWK (body block).
- Throw and block the 2-high SWK (double shield).

- From the 1-RK/brush-check. Counter with 2-3-RK.
- From the 1-RK/brush-check: Counter with 2-SWK (stepping back with the 2 to make room for a hard SWK).
- From the 1-2/brush-brush: Counter with 1-mid RK (to body).
- From the 1-2/brush-brush: Counter with 2-mid SWK (to body).
- From the 1-2/brush: Intercept the 2 with a JK. Follow with 1-2-mid SWK.
- From the 1-2/brush: Intercept the 2 with a JK. Follow with 2-3-low RK.
- From the 1-2/brush: Intercept the 2 with a JK. Follow with mid SWK-2.
- From the 1-2-3/brush-brush-body block: Counter with 3-low RK.
- From the 1-2-3/brush-brush-body block: Counter with 3-2-SWK (then step back into basic position).
- From the 1-2 high SWK/brush-brush-shield: Counter with 2-SWK.
- From the 1-2-high SWK/brush-brush-shield: Counter with 2-3-low RK.
- From the 1-2-high SWK/brush-brush-shield: Counter with 3-2-SWK to body.
- From 1-high RK/brush-shield: Counter with 3-2-high RK.
- From 1-2-high SWK/brush-brush-shield: Counter with 2-5-low RK.
- From 1-2-high SWK/brush-brush-shield: Counter with 2-low SWK.
- From 1-2-high SWK/brush-brush-shield: Counter with 2-high SWK.
- From 1-2-high SWK/brush-brush-shield: Counter with 1-low RK.
- From 1-2-high SWK/brush-brush-shield: Counter with 1-high RK.
- From 1-2-high SWK/brush-shield: Counter with 2-low SWK-2.
- From 1-2-high SWK/brush-shield: Counter with 2-high SWK-2.
- From 1-2/intercept with inside low leg kick: Follow up with 2-2-low RK.

- Block the 1-2: Counter with mid SWK-2-high SWK.
- Block the 1-2: Counter with JK-1-low RK. Grab same side of head and knee.
- Brush the 1-check the low SWK. Counter with low SWK-2-3. Grab and knee.
- Brush the 1-2-body block the mid SWK. Counter with 2-3-low RK.
- Brush and shield the 1-mid RK. Counter with mid RK-2-high SWK.
- Brush and shield the 1-2-high SWK. Counter with low SWK-2-high SWK.

In this sparring drill the fighter covers up to block the hook while reaching across to secure the grab and deliver a knee to the body.

In this drill the fighter slips the jab and simultaneously throws an inside leg kick.

In this sparring drill, the fighter brushes the jab and counters with a leg kick.

CLENCHING DRILLS WITH PARTNER

- Clench-spin-knee-escape (go back and forth, never letting go of clench).
- When you are close to the ropes and being rushed by an opponent, clench and spin to either direction.
- From the clench, lift the arm of your opponent and place a circle knee.
- From the clench, if your partner tries a circle knee, immediately spin him in the same direction of his knee attack. (Try this with your eyes closed).
- Practice clench escapes and placing light knee strikes.

SPARRING DRILLS

- Leg check or body block oncoming RK or SWK at different heights.
- Thai brush the jab; counter with a low RK, then grab the head on the right side and switch knee.
- Thai brush the right cross (2) into the long knee.[1]
- Catch and plow the RK into long knee.
- Catch the RK into a cut kick (the standing leg).
- 1-long knee.
- 1-2-switch knee.
- Thai brush the jab (1) and grab the head (right side) and switch knee.
- Thai brush the cross (2) and grab the head (left side) and long knee.
- Brush the 1-Thai brush the 2-into a long knee.
- From the 1-2-3 brush, brush body block and grab head (right) switch knee.
- Brush the 1-body block the 4-step in and long knee.
- Brush the 1-counter with an upward elbow grab (right) top of head and knee.

THAI PAD DRILLS USING BELLY PAD

- Jab kick-long knee (from charging opponent).
- Cross kick-left knee (keep right leg forward after the kick, then make the knee return to basic position).
- Circle knee slow (30 seconds)-skip knee slow (30 seconds)-circle knee/skip knee combination (right side 30 seconds/left side 30 seconds). Two-minute interval drill.
- Intercept partner's RK with a jab kick (to belly pad).
- Intercept the 1-2 with a jab kick (belly pad).
- Block the jab kick with a knee-counter with a right cross (2).
- Thai brush the (2) cross; counter with an elbow.
- Fake a jab-spin through with a backfist (right)-followed by an RK (to body)-clench and 5 to 10 skip knees.
- Slip outside partner's jab. Counter at the same time with a 7 (jab to body).
- Slip inside partner's jab. Simultaneously counter with 8-11 (right cross to body-left uppercut to body.
- Leg check partner's RK. Counter with 2-3-low RK (pad on back of leg)-step back (draw opponent in)-jab kick.
- Leg check partner's RK. Counter with 2-3-low RK (pad on back of leg)-step back (draw opponent in)-mid SWK.
- Body block partner's high SWK. Counter with 2-5-2-mid SWK-pivot out as partner rushes in.
- Body block partner's high RK. Counter with 2-mid SWK-pivot out as partner rushes in.
- Parry the JK inside. Counter with 3-mid RK-step back-2.
- Parry the JK outside-3-2-3-mid RK-step back (draw in opponent)-2.
- Shield the high RK. Counter with 3-long knee.
- Shield the high RK. Counter with 3-2-3-long knee-step back-high RK.

PUNCH SPARRING DRILLS WITH PARTNER

- 1 for 1.
- 2 for 2.
- 1-2 for 1-2.
- 3 for 3.
- 4 for 4.
- 5 for 5.
- 6 for 6.
- Same for all body punches "inside work."
- Brush the 1-2. Counter with 1-2-9-3 (short step back after combo).
- Brush the 1-2. Counter with 1-6-3-2-9 (short step back after combo).
- Brush the 1-2. Counter with 2-5-2-3 (short step back after combo).
- Brush the 1-2. Counter with 1-1-8-5-4.

EVASIONS AND COUNTERS (MITTS OR SPARRING)

- Slip the jab. Counter with 2-3-2.
- Slip the jab. Counter with 2-5-2-9.
- Slip the cross. Counter with 9-3-2-5-4.
- Brush the 1-2. Bob and weave the 3. Counter with 2-5-2-3.
- Brush, bob and weave the 1-4. Counter with 3-2-3.
- Slip and bob and weave the 1-2. Counter with 3-2.
- Bob and weave the 3-4 twice. Counter with 3-2-3.
- Fake the 2-throw the 9.
- Catch the uppercut. Counter with hook.
- Slip inside the 1. Counter (same time) with 8-3.

FOCUS MITT DRILLS AND TRAINING

- 1-1-2 going forward, coordinating the punches with the footwork.
- Partner rushes in; practice pivot and right cross. Counter (2).
- 1-2, 1-2-3, 1-2-3-6, 1-2-3-6-3, step back.
- 1, 1-6, 1-6-3, 1-6-3-2, step back.
- 2, 2-5, 2-5-2, 2-5-2-3, pivot.
- 3, 3-2, 3-2-3, 3-2-3 (step back catch partner coming in) with 2 , then pivot.
- 2, 2-3, 2-3-2, 2-3-2-3, pivot.
- 1-2, 1-2-9, 1-2-9-3, 1-2-9-3-2, step back.
- 2, 2-5, 2-5-2, 2-5-2-9, step back.
- Leg check the low RK; brush the 1. Counter with 1-2-3, grab and long knee.
- 1-2-3-2-BW-(R)-2-3.
- 1-2-3-BW-(L)-3-2.
- 6-3-BW.
- 5-4-BW.
- Pivot-drop-12-9.
- 5-4-BW (R) 9-10.
- From close in, use your lead shoulder to bump your opponent's shoulder, creating a quick opening for the 6-3 combination. Body block (L). Counter with 2-3.
- 1-slip the counterjab-step in with 6-3.
- 1-brush the counterjab-follow with double jab (1-1).
- 1-brush the counterjab-follow with double jab and cross (1-1-2).
- 1-7.
- 7-1.
- 1-2.
- 1-8.
- 7-2.
- 1-2-3.
- 7-8.
- 1-3.
- 1-8-3.
- 8-3.
- 2-3.
- 2-9.
- 1-2-BW-2.
- 1-1-2-3-2.
- 1-2-5-2-3.
- Body block (L)-6-3.
- Body block (R)-5-4.
- 1-2-1.
- 1-slip. BW (from 1-2)-finish with 3.
- Brush the 1-2. Body block the high SWK, counter quickly with 3-2.
- Fast 1, soft 4 to hide the simultaneous low RK.
- Fake the 1, throw the 2.
- Slip outside the 1, counter same time with your own 1 (jab).

Here is a sample focus mitt drill. The trainer drills the fighter on the jab, cross, left hook combination (1-2-3) and then counterpunches with a right hook (4) as the fighter covers, grabs, and finishes with a knee.

SPARRING ELBOW DRILLS WITH PARTNER

Practice with a partner: One throws as the other blocks for a round, and vice versa. Can be performed with pads or in stand-alone sparring drills.

- Hooking elbow (left and right).
- Upward elbow.
- Downward elbow.
- Diagonal elbow.
- Thai brush the 1-counter with left elbow.
- Thai brush the 2-counter with right elbow.
- Body block the hook off both sides countering with elbow, grab top of head and knee.
- Fake a hooking elbow left and step through and deliver a spinning elbow.
- Leg check the low RK-step in with the right elbow.
- Jab-right elbow.
- Jab-left elbow.
- 1-2-3-right elbow.
- 1-2-upward elbow (left).
- 1-2-upward elbow (left), hooking elbow (right).
- Spar with all elbows from the clench position.

PUNCH AND ELBOW MITT TRAINING

- 6-3-RE.
- 6-3-RE-step back-2-LE.
- 1-2-9-RE.
- 1-2-9-RE-step back-LUE.
- 1-2-3-right spinning elbow.

COMBINATION SPARRING DRILLS

The following drills can be done with a sparring partner or on the Thai pads.

- 1-RK (punch is used to blind opponent to the kick).
- 3-RK (draw the hands up with the hook, opening the body for the kick).
- 5-RK (step around, kick around, and down).
- 1-2-SWK.

- 1-6-SWK.
- 2-3-low RK.
- 1-2-5-RK.
- 1-fake the 2-SWK.
- 1-fake the RK-SWK around.
- 1-fake the RK-follow through with RK (draw the lead leg up with the fake and deliver kick to the standing leg).
- Brush the 1-2. Counter with 1-RK.
- Brush the 1-2. Counter with low RK.
- Brush the 1-2. Counter with 2 (distraction)-low RK.
- Brush the 1-2. Counter with inside leg kick (all one movement, brush and inside leg kick).
- Interrupt a slow RK with a faster one of your own.
- Interrupt a SWK with one of your own (posting with your left hand).
- Cut kick drill (interrupt a high RK with a sweeping low SWK and vice versa).
- Shield partner's high RK and counter with low RK.
- Shield the high SWK. Counter with low SWK.
- Brush the 1. Counter with low RK.

PARRY AND REDIRECT PARTNER DRILLS

- Parry the jab kick inside (toward the centerline of the body).
- Parry the jab kick outside (away from the centerline of the body).
- Parry the cross kick inside (toward the centerline of the body).
- Parry the cross kick outside (away from the centerline of the body).

PARRY AND COUNTER DRILLS

- Parry the JK inside. Counter with low RK, grab top of head and knee.
- Parry the JK inside. Counter with low RK. Post with right hand-high SWK.
- Parry the JK inside. Counter with mid or high RK (partner shields/body block).
- Parry the JK outside. Counter with mid SWK-2-3-low RK.

- Parry the JK outside. Counter with low, mid, or high SWK (partner block/shield).
- Parry the JK outside. Counter with 3-2-mid SWK (look for fluid transitions).
- Parry the JK outside. Counter with 3-low RK. Post with right hand and high SWK.
- Parry the JK outside. Counter with 2-mid SWK.

PARRY THE CROSS KICK DRILLS

- Parry the CK inside. Counter with low, mid, or high SWK.
- Parry the CK inside. Counter with low SWK-2-3-high RK.
- Parry the CK inside. Counter with 2 (parrying hand)-low SWK-1-grab (right side) and switch knee.
- Parry the CK outside. Counter with 2-post with left hand-low SWK (to inside leg).

SHIELD AND PARRY DRILLS

Shield and parry drills use double-forearm blocking and redirecting just like in the parry, and teach you to guard for middle and high round kicks. To redirect to the right, use the right hand; to redirect left, use the left hand. (See Chapter 2.)

- Shield and parry the mid SWK. Counter with low RK. Grab and switch knee.
- Shield and parry the mid SWK. Counter with 3-2-mid SWK.
- Shield and parry the high RK. Counter with low SWK-2-low SWK.
- Shield and parry the mid RK. Counter with 2-1-(post)-mid RK.
- Shield and parry the high RK. Counter with mid RK.
- Shield and parry the high SWK. Counter with low RK-3-low RK.
- Shield and parry (down) the high SWK. Counter with 3-2-mid SWK.
- Shield and parry (down) the high SWK. Counter with high SWK-2.
- Shield and parry (down) the high SWK. Counter with low SWK-2-mid or high SWK.

Sample Beginner Workouts
- Four rounds of punching (mitts).
- Three rounds of counterkicks (Thai pads).
- Two rounds of knee work (Thai pads).
- Three rounds of sparring.
- Fifty power kicks with the left leg.
- Fifty power kicks with the right leg.

TRAINING METHODS

Straight Rounds
Work the bag or Thai pads for a three-minute round with continuous intensity. Try to build up your stamina so that you can hit with full power for the entire round. You can increase your intensity and stamina by shortening the rest time between rounds, increasing your striking speed, trying new kick-and-punch combinations, or increasing the overall number of rounds.

Bag Intervals
Work at a steady but moderate pace for the first 15 seconds. At the 15-second bell go all out with nonstop power punches or kicks. Alternate between moderate and intense activity for the entire round.

Carry Bag
A realistic and powerful exercise is known as carry-bag training. Simply use a heavy bag that is at least 4 feet long (a 6-foot bag is also great) and is not suspended from the ceiling. At the start of the round, pick up the bag and hold it in a low clench position. You keep the bag up for the entire round and practice striking it with knees. This is very exhausting but simulates the experience of fighting in a clench while developing great endurance in the leg, hip, back, and arm muscles. There is no better way (save for hard sparring in the clench with a partner) to prepare for the intensity of fighting in this manner.

Partner Intervals
With one person on either side of the bag, alternate hard interval rounds—one person works while the other rests. Utilizing the *work-rest method*, you will alternate between rest and

Paul Brymer works the carry bag.

interval (1-2-3-RK, or clench and knee). Alternate between offense and defense during the round.

Thai Pad Conditioning

The pad holder will call out a number between 1 and 5. The number he calls out represents the number of punches to be thrown for that combination (see the chart below). Each punch or combination is followed by a round or switch kick (going left to right or right to left depending on from which side the last punch was thrown). Some simple punch combinations for this drill are as follows:

- 1 = Jab-round kick
- 2 = Jab-right cross-switch kick
- 3 = Jab-right cross-left hook-round kick
- 4 = Jab-right cross-left hook-right cross-switch kick
- 5 = Jab-right cross-left uppercut-right cross-left hook-round kick

With some practice you and the pad holder will develop a good rhythm, and your punch and kick combinations should improve in speed, power, and fluidity. You will always feel tired after these types of rounds if you hit full power. When you are in shape, however, you will hit just as hard during the entire round, even though you will be breathing hard. Doing three to six rounds is not only great for building stamina but also for making your combinations come more naturally.

Focus Mitt Intervals

Set an interval timer for 30-second intervals. Work each punch beginning with the 1 (jab) and going through the 6 (right uppercut), changing punches at each 30-second period.

Active Rest

Active rest involves doing calisthenics exercise in place of rest periods in between training rounds on the bag or pads. For example, work three rounds straight on Thai pads with calisthenics (push-ups, lunges, squat-thrusts, crunches) in between rounds.

all-out intensity. You can work for 30-second or one-minute intervals, resting one period and working at full intensity for the next.

Thai Pad Intervals

Thai pad intervals can utilize full-power training, test defensive skills, and provide constant physical and psychological pressure. Set the timer to 15- or 30-second intervals and work at a moderate pace for the first period. Set an all-out 100 percent pace for the next, continuing to vary the intensity from medium to heavy at each interval period.

For example, begin with all-out punches for the first 30-second interval. At the bell go to all-out skip knees for 30 seconds. Repeat working the punch combos hard for 30 seconds, then the knee hard for 30 seconds until the end of the round.

Work 30 seconds on individual kicks non-stop (jab, cross, round, and switch kicks). As the 30-second interval changes, you go to a different kick, working on delivering the kick with speed and power.

Concentrate on defense for one period, blocking your partner's attacks and hitting the pads hard with a set combination during the

Pyramid Sets on RK/SWK or SKN

Begin by throwing one round kick, switch kick, or knee (from the clench) with full power. Then after a deep breath throw two, rest a moment then three, four, and so on until you reach 10. Do not rush the exercise: Throw each strike with full deliberate power; don't sacrifice form and power by making it into a race.

Circuit Training

Circuit training includes moving from one station to another with little rest between rounds. For example, pick a few conditioning exercises and mix with bag rounds and sparring to set up a good circuit. Set a workout timer for two to three minutes with 30 seconds to one minute of rest. After completing each sequence of rounds repeat one to three times.

- Round 1: Jump rope
- Round 2: Bag round
- Round 3: 30 crunches/30 push-ups
- Round 4: Sparring
- Round 5: Shadowboxing
- Round 6: Knee work on Thai pads
  Repeat 3X

- Round 1: Round kicks on Thai pads
- Round 2: Shadowboxing
- Round 3: Squats
- Round 4: Double-end bag
- Round 5: 30 crunches/50 squat thrusts
- Round 6: Sparring
  Repeat 3X

- Round 1: Combinations on punch mitts
- Round 2: Kick combinations on the bag
- Round 3: 30 sit-ups/10 folds
- Round 4: Sparring with the clench, light knees
- Round 5: Jump rope
- Round 6: Bag round
  Repeat 3X

- Round 1: Dips (30 seconds)
- Round 2: Sit-ups (30 seconds)
- Round 3: Pull-ups (30 seconds)
- Round 4: Jump squats (30 seconds)

- Round 5: Power kicks on the bag (1 minute)
- Round 6: Push-ups (30 seconds)
- Round 7: Sit-ups (30 seconds)
- Round 8: Curls (30 seconds)
- Round 9: Jump squats (30 seconds)
- Round 10: Shadowbox (1 minute)
  Repeat 3X

Basic Boxing Workout Program

All rounds are two minutes long with 30 seconds of rest in between. Warm up for five minutes and stretch for 10 minutes before beginning. Follow up with abdominal work and 20 minutes of stretching.

- Three rounds shadowboxing
- Three or four rounds of sparring
- Three rounds heavy bag
- Three rounds double-end bag
- Three rounds jump rope
- Three rounds punch mitts
- Three rounds speed bag

Thai Boxing Workout Program

All rounds are three minutes with one minute of rest. Stretch for five minutes before beginning and follow up with five minutes of abdominal work.

- Three rounds on the punch mitts
- Three rounds on the Thai pads
- Five rounds of sparring
- Two rounds of sparring in the clench
- Fifty round kicks (each leg) on the bag

Thai Boxing Workout Program

All rounds are three minutes with one minute of rest. Begin with five minutes of stretching and end with five minutes of abdominal work.

- Two rounds working the knee from the clench on the Thai pads
- Three interval rounds on the bag (15- or 30-second intervals)
- Five rounds of sparring
- One hundred round kicks on the bag for each leg

Thai Boxing Workout Program

All rounds are three minutes with one minute of rest.

Circuit Training

- One round working straight kicks on the big pad
- One round working round kicks on the Thai pads while blocking the pad holder's attacks
- One round punch combination on mitts
- One round sparring
- One round on the bag
- One round slipping and evading punches or kicks

Conditioning (No Rest)

- One minute squat thrusts
- One minute crunches
- One minute push-ups
- One minute crunches
- One minute jump squats

Interval Training

- Three rounds of 15-second bag intervals
- One round of Thai pad intervals

Sparring

- Five rounds of sparring

Running

- Run for 20 to 30 minutes

• • •

1. The long knee refers to using the right (or back) leg, as opposed to the switch knee, which uses the left (or lead) leg and requires you to switch feet to make room for a powerful knee strike.

Advice for the Novice Fighter

*Once men are caught up in an event, they cease
to be afraid. Only the unknown frightens men.*
—Antoine de Saint-Exupery
1900-1944

After a few years of hard training, you may want to consider the challenge of fighting in the ring. While fighting is not for everyone, there is no greater test of your mental strength, physical conditioning, skills, and character than to compete in the ring. Fighting offers the reward of real confidence and is great for those who thrive on challenge and pressure. Some may even travel overseas and fight all over the world. Unless you aspire to ascend to world-class level, the financial rewards of fighting in the ring will not measure up to the work involved. But even competing on a local level can earn you a collection of trophies, belts, pictures, and memories to exaggerate about as the years pass. The experience of fighting in local and regional boxing, kickboxing, Muay Thai, and NHB is an incredible one. There are some things to consider and beware of, however.

BE PREPARED

There are several things to consider when thinking about fighting in the ring. These include your goals, your preparation, and your management. Do you want to become professional or do you simply thrive on challenge and want to compete in a few local fights? Are you prepared both physically, mentally, and emotionally? Do you have competent managers and trainers that you can trust? When answering these questions, don't trust what anybody tells you—make your judgments based on people's actions.

Keep in mind that, unless you aspire to be a world champion, you should put fighting in its place. Always fight to win, but remember that

Some keepsakes of the fight game.

losing a match is not the end of the world. As long as you know that you did your best, you really shouldn't feel bad at the end of the day. The confidence that comes from having the courage it takes to fight is its own reward. You will win and you will lose, but how you feel afterward about your performance is important.

For example, I once won a match by TKO when my opponent dislocated his shoulder throwing a wild punch. Even though I got a win, I knew that I wasn't in shape and had not prepared for this fight correctly. On the other end of the spectrum I later lost a fight but felt great afterward because I had trained hard and had been prepared. I knocked my opponent down four times in three different rounds, and in the third round he actually turned his back and ran away! After having one of my best fights, I lost a controversial split decision. Things won't always go your way, but always do your best.

How well have you prepared for the fight? Many talented and hardworking fighters simply don't respond to the pressure of being in front of a crowd for the first time. Many new fighters are great in the gym, paying their proverbial dues and showing confidence and skill in sparring. These same guys can freeze up in their first match because of self-doubt and the nervousness that comes from being in front of the crowd. Experience breeds confidence, and fighters usually improve with each fight. Everyone who has ever stepped between the ropes has a real perspective that no armchair quarterback ever will.

Finally, you don't always get what you deserve; you get what you negotiate. Promoters want to get fighters in the ring, and some are more trustworthy than others. Sometimes young, amateur fighters with no ring experience are thrown in over their heads, fighting grossly

A fighter delivers a round kick to his opponent's head. Photo by Zoran Rebac, from his book Thai Boxing Dynamite *(Paladin Press).*

MUAY THAI KICKBOXING

overmatched opponents at the last minute. Many times I have seen promoters lie about another fighter's abilities and record just to convince someone to get in the ring with him. You have to put your own interests first because no one is going to do it for you. Make sure that you are comfortable with all of the stipulations of the fight. Don't agree at the last minute to fight five rounds if you have only trained for a three-round bout. Don't agree to fight someone other than your scheduled opponent unless you are confident that you are prepared. If someone backed out of a fight there may have been good reason.

An important part of the game is to let others you trust make the decisions for you on fight night. Your opponent may want to fight with or without headgear or shinguards at the last minute or want to change some rules of the fight that will favor him. Your corner knows your strengths and weaknesses and is better suited to accept or decline these sorts of last minute changes. I once agreed at the last minute to fight with heavily padded gloves (instead of the original broken-in 12-ounce ones) against a fighter who knew I had a reputation for hard punches. This was a stupid decision that I should have let my corner make for me. When you are mentally focused on the opponent you are less likely to be objective and make rational decisions. The ego can get in the way of reasonable thought. Let your corner men do their job outside the ring as well as inside it.

The fight game is rewarding in many ways but can be disillusioning in others, especially when it comes to pro events. If you are offered a pro fight, be sure to agree to the dollar amount first. (Also, a contract is always a plus.) For example, I cornered for a friend once and we were assigned the one-stall men's room as a warm-up area. Because this was a pro fight I did my best to get the guy ready in a room the size of a box that was reeking of piss and sweat. The end of the night came. I went to talk to the promoter about getting my friend his pay (which would have conveniently been forgotten). I was handed a stack of twenties to give to the main-event fighter, what should have been a hundred bucks or so. On the way home (a four-hour drive) a closer inspection of the pay revealed that it was a $20 wrapped around five $1s—a slap in the face.

The point here is not to scare you away from the ring; it is to enlighten you to some things that go on. Fighting in the ring is an exhilarating challenge, but you must be prepared for anything.

Stalking an opponent in the ring.

The first blow is half the battle.
—Oliver Goldsmith
1728-1774

TIPS FOR FIGHT TIME

Surround yourself with positive influences. You must control your mind; it is easy to let self-doubt creep in at the last minute. It helps if you surround yourself with positive, knowledgeable people backstage. I remember I brought my dad along for my first fight and, God bless him, he meant well but he came in and told me, "Chad, (your opponent) looks pretty serious. You sure about this?" (I'm not sure what look he was expecting to see in my opponent's expression. Humor, boredom, bedroom eyes?) Your mind is your most important weapon; don't become your own worst enemy.

Focus your mind. Mental focus is the most important thing before a match. Sometimes opponents will try to break your focus in hopes of shaking your confidence, and you can't let them.

Train your mind and your body. Weeks before the fight you can begin preparing your mind with visualization and burnouts.

Elite athletes use *visualization*, or mental imagery, to prepare for competition. In your mind, create the scenario that you want to happen in the ring. See and feel everything that will take place. Recall the feeling you had after your best sparring match—the confidence you felt—and relive it as you see yourself knocking out your opponent. Do this each day leading up to the big fight. When you are actually in the ring staring down your opponent, you won't be staring him down for the first time.

Another way of garnering confidence several weeks before a fight is to do *burnouts* during your bag rounds or runs in training. When running at a steady pace, take off and sprint until you feel that you are completely out of gas (30 seconds should do it), and then continue on at your usual pace. Use the same technique when working the bag. Pace yourself as usual and then go all-out for 30 seconds or so. When you feel you can't go on, go on. In a fight, you must sprint or give all-out bursts of energy, so do it in training. Losing your breath and then getting it back is imperative for your confidence. The only better confidence-builder is ring experience, and you will have that in time.

Relax, but not too much. First-fight butterflies are normal, so don't let them control you. Turn the nervousness into focus when you are in the ring. Use deep, controlled breathing to help calm the nerves. Inhale for four to five counts; exhale as slowly as possible. This method of breathing can also help you recover quickly in between rounds.

Be active in the ring. Don't wait for your opponent to knock himself out; he won't. Do what you do in sparring and let the punches fly, but don't get sloppy and drop your guard. Keep calm, focused, and aggressive.

Avoid freezing up. Many fighters freeze up in their first fight; this is normal. A good way to avoid this is to spar in the gym the way you plan to fight. For example, when an opponent charges forward and your instinct is to back up, train yourself to throw a right hand or a quick round kick to the leg instead.

Be confident, but not overconfident. You must believe in yourself, but too much of a good thing is poisonous. After winning a boxing tournament by way of four consecutive knockouts, I was feeling pretty confident. So after sitting on my couch for a few weeks I agreed to a fight a five-rounder on a week's notice. It was a bad idea; I had not trained for the fight. I thought that I was good enough to fight right off the couch—massive ego strikes again. My diabetes was out of control and I was mentally unprepared. My opponent was not. Lesson learned.

Outthink your opponent. Play the game using your style—do what you are best at when sparring in the gym. Some fighters are counterpunchers who fight well when defensive, while others are better when they are super-aggressive. Fight according to your own unique talents and skills.

Be in shape. This is 80+ percent of combat sports. Many talented and skilled athletes simply run out of gas in a tough fight. Imagine your body moving in slow motion, both legs feeling like they weigh a ton, while your opponent looks fresh. This is not what you want to happen in the last round! Proper training and conditioning always pays off in the ring.

Keep hydrated. Drink plenty of water in the weeks leading up to the fight. Sports drinks are also useful, as they provide electrolytes and minerals to aid performance.

Stick to the basics. A fight is not the right place to try new moves or complicated combinations that you aren't completely comfortable with yet. Simple, basic moves like the jab, cross, hook, and round kick (1-2-3-RK) are the best bets. Keep the attacks simple and the pressure on your opponent constant.

Styles make fights. Scout your opponent whenever possible, watch tapes, and get feedback from people who know his style. A good coach will be able to help you prepare an appropriate game plan according to your opponent's strengths and weaknesses. Does your fighter prefer to get close and slug it out, or does he stay outside and kick? This type of information can be important in developing your own strategy.

Appear confident. Show confidence at all times. Do not show weaknesses such as pain or fatigue. Your appearance to the crowd and the judges (not to mention your opponent) during the fight and in between rounds is important. I make it a point to stand up between rounds to appear as though I am not tired (whether I am or not). Answering punches (hitting the opponent right back if he gets a punch on you) is also an important tactic to minimize the appearance of damage.

Lead with straights. Use the jab and cross aggressively and often because they are safe leads and good setups. You can also use them to catch a rushing opponent. Don't wait for the perfect time, because there may not be one. Throw the straight punches often.

Keep moving. Move steadily; a moving target is harder to hit. However, do not waste energy "jumping around" unnecessarily. Sidestep a rushing opponent rather than backing up, which could make your opponent look dominant in the ring. Lastly, cut off the ring. This is done by not letting your opponent circle around you. Sidestep with your opponent, blocking his path of escape. The object is to cut him off and force him into the ropes or into a corner where he has nowhere to go.

Maintain a good stance. Keep your hands up and chin tucked in at all times. This basic positioning can easily be forgotten in the heat of a fight.

Learn your range. Punch and kick when your opponent is in range or moving forward at you. Measure that range with your jab.

Vary your attack. Avoid being predictable; do not use the same combinations over and over. It is easy to get someone's timing when each attack is the same as the last. If you feel your opponent is reading you like a book and is a few pages ahead, then change something!

Set up the next move. Use the punches to set up the leg kicks and the leg kicks to set up the punches.

Keep your balance. Continually try to put your opponent off-balance. An off-balance fighter looks bad to the judges and is susceptible to more damaging blows.

Work on your accuracy. Try to hit more often in lieu of hitting hard. A weaker kick or punch that hits the target is better than a powerful one that misses.

Maintain eye contact. Always look straight at your opponent. The eyes are a good focal point. Keep your mouth shut over your mouthpiece to protect your teeth

Learn to sidestep. Move sideways and forward to get close. Step outside the opponent's lead hand (jab). Take short steps when jabbing.

Practice feinting. Faking punches or kicks is beneficial as long as you have practiced it in the gym. The idea is to confuse and distract the opponent. For example, fake a jab and throw a right hand when the opponent reacts.

Don't waste energy. Try to relax the body except when throwing the punch and kick.

Don't warm up too soon. After arriving on time for the fight (usually an hour or two early), go somewhere to relax. Begin physically warming up about 15 minutes or so before your match. Avoid strength movements such as push-ups and sit-ups. Work on shadowboxing, footwork, or sparring drills with your coach.

FIGHTER'S GEAR

Boxing license/picture ID
Handwraps/bag gloves
Groin protector
Fighting shorts
Robe
Mouthpiece
Shin pads
Foot pads
Headgear
Jump rope
Warm-up sweats
Boxing and cross-training shoes

CORNERMAN'S GEAR

Petroleum jelly
Gauze and tape
Cotton swabs
Ice packs
Water bottles
Bandages
Scissors
Bucket
Antiseptic
Towels
Water

Some moderate basic pad work can be good before the fight to get the blood pumping.

Eat light. Many fighters have a hard time eating before a fight due to nerves. A light meal two hours before a fight is helpful because you want some food in your system to avoid hunger pangs. If you feel you need something as fight time approaches, eat a light snack but avoid filling up. The day before the fight make sure to get plenty of carbohydrates (potatoes, pasta, vegetables).

Learn from your losses and victories. Looking at tapes of your fights and getting feedback from your team will give you the best idea of what you need to work on in the gym to make your next fight better. Improve yourself every time you step in the ring, and you are a true success, win or lose.

Remember to bring all your gear. Make a checklist and pack the day before you leave to eliminate any last-minute worries. If you are fighting out of town and staying the night, then you will need to remember to pack personal items as well.

WEIGHT CLASSES

Kickboxing, NHB, and boxing separate fighters by weight. Determine what weight class you want to compete in early on so that you can train accordingly. The weight classes are detailed in the following list. Depending on the fight promoter and sanctioning body, the weight classes may vary.

- Super heavyweight: More than 210 pounds
- Heavyweight: 190 to 209 pounds
- Cruiserweight: 180 to 189 pounds
- Light heavyweight: 169 to 179 pounds
- Super middleweight: 161 to 168 pounds
- Middleweight: 155 to 160 pounds
- Light middleweight: 148 to 154 pounds
- Welterweight: 143 to 147 pounds
- Super lightweight: 138 to 142 pounds
- Lightweight: 133 to 137 pounds
- Featherweight: 125 to 132 pounds
- Bantamweight: 120 to 124 pounds
- Flyweight: 117 to 119 pounds
- Atomweight: Less than 117 pounds

TOUGHMAN BOXING WEIGHT CLASSES

- Heavyweight: 185 pounds and above
- Middleweight: 165 to 185 pounds
- Lightweight: 145 to 165 pounds

STYLES AND STRATEGIES

Against a Taller Opponent
- To negate his reach advantage, try to make the taller fighter come to you.
- Slip the taller opponent's straight punches while moving in behind your jab and follow up with punch combinations and low kicks.

- Utilize multiple leg kicks to take the bigger man's power away; it is better to land 10 leg kicks at 50 percent of your power than to land only one at 100 percent.
- Try to cut the ring off by backing the taller opponent into the ropes and staying in his face.
- Punch to the liver (a left hook to the body for conventional fighters) when close. This is good for taking away an opponent's power and will.

Against a Rushing Fighter
- Sidestep and work the right cross or low round kick. Don't move straight back.
- Use the lead leg kick to the inside thigh to disrupt his balance and forward momentum.
- If the rusher gets inside, keep your elbows in and hands up, rolling your spine a little to make your arms cover more of your body (do not look away—you must keep your eyes on the opponent). Make sure to move in close to take away your opponent's punching room.
- If the opponent seems to be a better boxer, keep your elbows high and clench him to stop his punches.
- Do not hesitate to throw the jab and right cross hard at a rushing opponent.

Against a Shorter Opponent
- A shorter fighter must get close to you to hit you, so use the straight punches often.
- Do not step forward; sidestep and keep the shorter fighter at a distance.
- Punch in combination and finish with low kicks.
- Only kick high if your opponent is hurt or visibly tired. A savvy fighter will sweep your legs out from under you if you throw too many high kicks.

Against a Jabber
- Use the right hand to catch or brush the jabs.
- Slip and evade and move in to work the body; your footwork should move you outside the opponent's jab.
- Cut the ring off and do not let him advance or sidestep; try to force him/her into the ropes to get close range.
- Thai brush the jab and drive in hard leg kicks when his balance is disrupted.

Against a Slugger
- Keep moving constantly. Don't allow your opponent to get his feet planted.
- Move in quickly and throw fast combinations.
- Don't get suckered into a slugfest—just box.

Boxing a Left-Handed Fighter
- Make your opponent come to you.
- Circle to your left and keep your right hand up to catch his powerful left hand.
- Hook off your jab often; the left hook (3) is a powerful weapon.
- Use your lead leg round kick often.

FIGHTING TO SURVIVE: MUAY THAI OUTSIDE THE RING

Not everyone who takes up combat sports training aspires to compete in the ring. Many people take up training in martial arts to learn to effectively defend themselves in an increasingly violent world. Many of these people are women that want to protect themselves and for good reason:

- According to a January 2000 report released by the National Victims Center, an estimated 67 out of every 100,000 females in the United States were reported rape victims in 1998.
- It is estimated that one woman in three is sexually assaulted in her lifetime.
- Every minute in America there are 1.3 forcible rapes of adult women.
- Every day muggings, assaults, rapes, carjacking, thefts, and burglaries take place in this country.
- According to the FBI, approximately 80 percent of sexual assault victims knew their assailants at least by sight. Sixty-one percent of sexual assault victims are under the age of 18, and 22 percent are between the ages of 18 and 24.

Regardless of your sex, if you are attacked in the street, there are no rules; your assailant may have a weapon or friends nearby. He may want to rape, mutilate, kidnap, or kill you and you must not hold anything back. Once a physical altercation has begun, it is time for war. Forget any so-called expert who tells you to attempt to talk your way out or to use minimum force to escape. Some may rationalize that fighting back may anger an attacker. However, FBI surveys with violent criminals found that only 1 percent of violent criminals indicated that this was the case. The decision to hurt you has already been made.

Despite the fact that you may not be an aggressive or violent person by nature, you must be willing to kill in order to save your own life.

You cannot depend on others to assist you in a situation or even care if you are being attacked (until they are comfortably watching the story at home on the news, or discussing it with friends). It is a sad fact, but many rape prevention and defense specialists actually teach women that it is preferable to scream "FIRE" instead of "RAPE." The reason: People may actually turn their head to look at a fire, but most people are too self-absorbed or afraid to get involved in helping an attack victim. The point is that everyone today must take responsibility for his or her own safety. This section covers fighting techniques to protect you in the street. We will go over some scenarios that incorporate some Thai boxing and grappling in common self-defense situations.

First off, it is important to note that it's always best to prevent an assault before it can happen. The following general self-defense combat tips and concepts are important, especially for women:

- Be aware of your surroundings at all times. Jog or travel around well-known safe areas.
- If possible, carry a cell phone.
- According to the U.S. Department of Justice, 25 percent of violent crimes occur near the home. Many car accidents occur less than one mile from home as well. One reason is that when we are close to home we tend to let our guard down. Remain aware.
- Carry yourself in a confident manner. Body language gives off signals, and one who walks while looking at the ground, or with thoughts elsewhere, makes an easy target. And make no mistake, a criminal is looking for an easy target.

- Beware of taking a fight to the ground intentionally. Even though there are skilled grapplers, male and female, who can subdue or choke out an untrained opponent, the ground may be the worst place to be if there are multiple attackers. The hard concrete, broken glass, and other objects could work against you.
- Do not hesitate to attack. Understand that you are in a kill-or-be-killed situation. You must fight fast and hard. Stun or hurt the attacker and get away.
- Strike the sensitive areas such as the eyes, throat, and groin fast and hard. In the street use your fingers to gouge the eyes and the heel of your hand to punch the throat.
- Expect that you will get hurt. Fight with all you have and never give up. Remember that the most dangerous animal is a cornered or wounded one.
- Use basic techniques such as gouging the eyes with your fingers, clenching the head, kneeing the groin and face, and striking with elbows to the chin, nose, temple, and throat.
- Taking self-defense courses can be beneficial. These courses put on by police, women's groups, and self-defense instructors can raise your awareness and provide tips for conflict avoidance. Beware, however, that effective physical self-defense must become second nature; this comes with repetition. I have often heard people claim, "I don't need to learn or practice anything. I could hurt someone if I had to." Unfortunately, in reality this is almost never the case. Consistent practice with basic techniques in a realistic attack situation is a must: You will always fight in the same manner as you train.
- From a frontal confrontation keep the hands up and act in a submissive manner. This makes the attacker feel psychologically in control, but in reality it is the best defensive and offensive position for your hands.

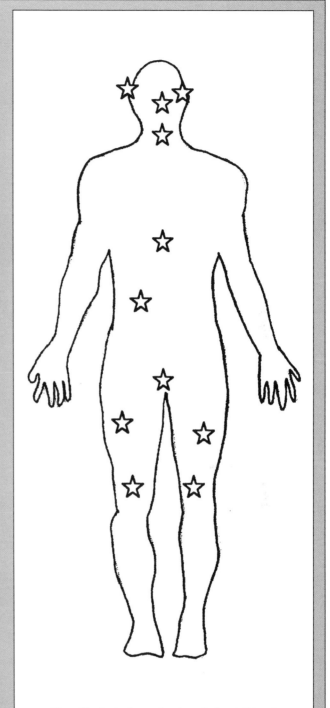

Stars illustrate damaging targets for striking in dangerous conflicts. The eyes, nose, throat, solar plexus (just below the center of the ribcage), liver, groin, thighs, and behind the ear are potentially devastating strike zones in self-defense situations.

In a frontal confrontation, kickboxer Tara Romano keeps her hands up and acts in a submissive manner.

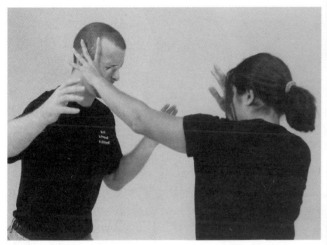

Strike quickly with a jab, driving a finger or thumb into the attacker's eyes.

If he strikes or grabs at you, cover and cross-grab with the other hand.

Pull his head down as you knee to the groin.

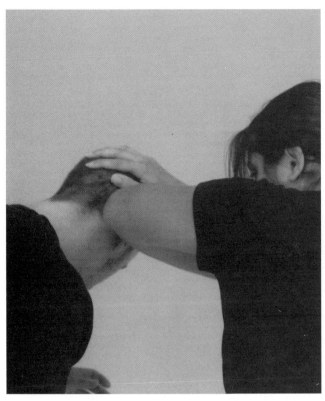

Strike him hard behind the ear with the point of your elbow.

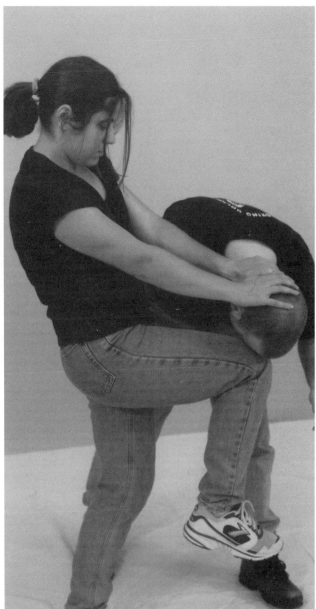

Drive knees into his face as needed and escape.

Pivot to one side and completely straighten your arms, holding his head down with your weight on both hands.

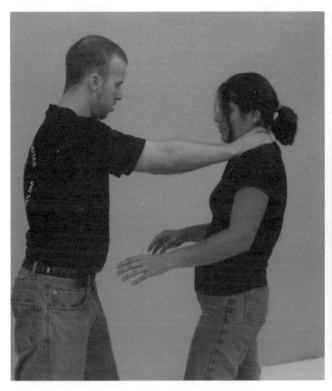

The attacker grabs your shirt or throat from the front.

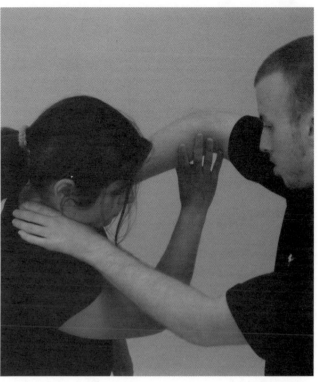

Use the elbow shove: Slap one elbow inside to make room to slide your opposite arm up the middle and grab the back of his head.

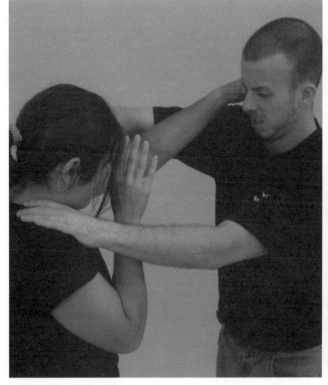

While sliding your hand up the middle, drive your thumb into his eye.

Once you have a grip, smash his nose with your forehead.

MUAY THAI KICKBOXING

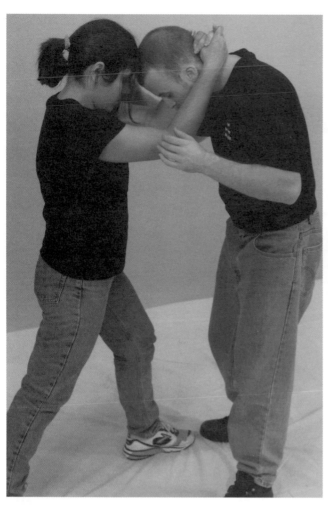

Get both hands on the top of his head and pull for a clench.

Drive knees into the groin.

He may resist and pull his head backward to escape.

In this case, keep your grip with the closest hand and drive an elbow into his chin or nose with the other.

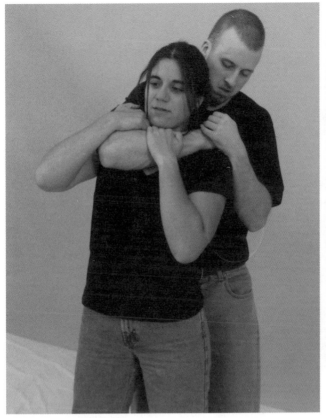

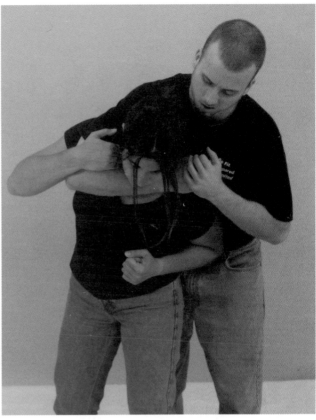

If you are grabbed from behind, put your fingers between the attacker's forearm and your throat to allow some breathing room.

Try to make a little space with an elbow strike to the body.

Get your hips directly under his hips by squatting, and keep your grip on the attacker's arm. Keep your head up.

Explode up at the knees and drive your hips upward under his. This will take him a few inches off his feet.

Turn him over your hip while jerking his arm across your body in the same direction.

MUAY THAI KICKBOXING

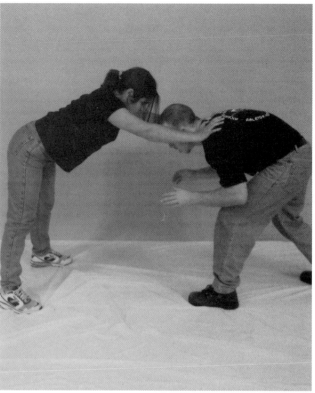

The attacker tries to tackle you by charging forward low.

Sprawl back by driving your weight down on him with your arms and quickly bringing your feet back.

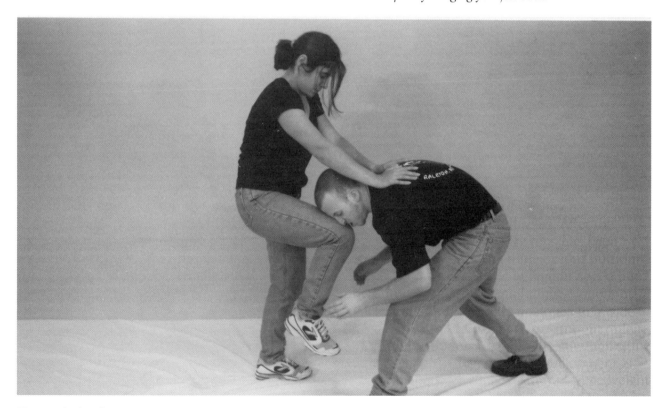

Knee to the head.

The attacker grabs from the rear.

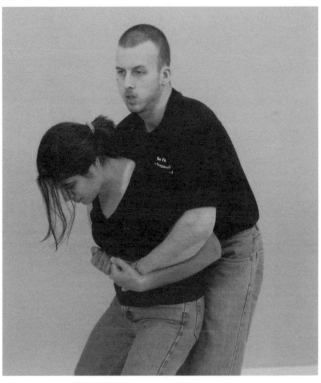

Drop your body weight while securing his hands.

Make room by striking with an elbow to his throat or chin from behind.

Push out and turn toward him, grasping his head.

MUAY THAI KICKBOXING

Throw a knee strike to the eye, nose, or jaw.

Sink your hips down as you bend your elbow, leaving no space between your arm and his throat. Then straighten your legs and drive the hips forward as you tighten the choke, pulling the forearm up and bending the attacker's head down by arching your back.

Slide your arm down one side of his throat and lean your weight on him.

1. The attacker cocks back for a punch.

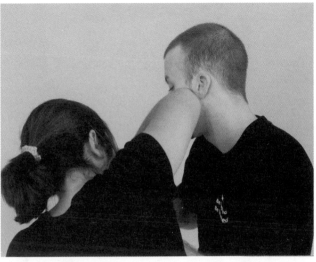

3. Then a right downward elbow to the face.

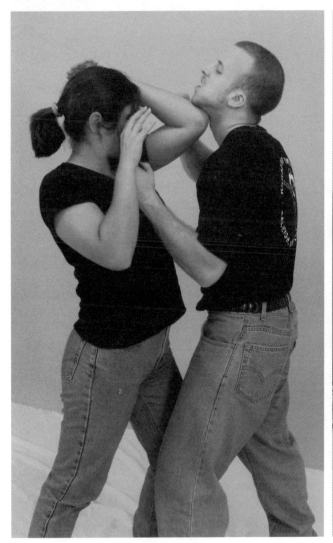

2. Step in with a left upward elbow.

4. Step around and grab the back of his head

MUAY THAI KICKBOXING

5. Knee to the face or throat.

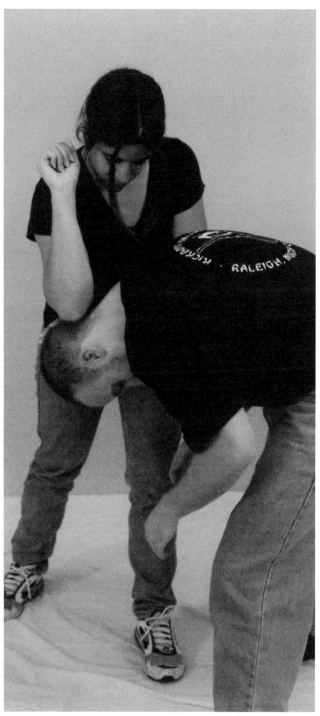

7. And finish with an elbow to the base of the skull.

6. Keep your weight on his head and raise your opposite arm.

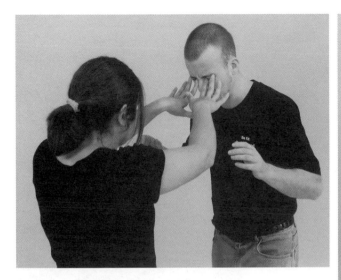

1. As the attacker advances, gouge his eyes.

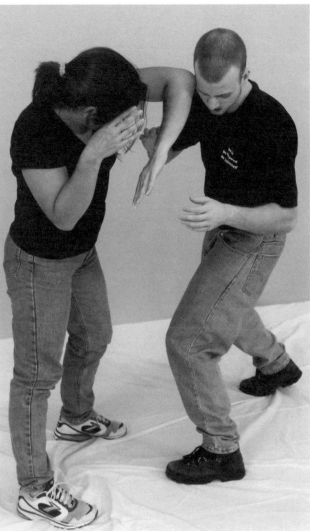

3. A hard overhand elbow.

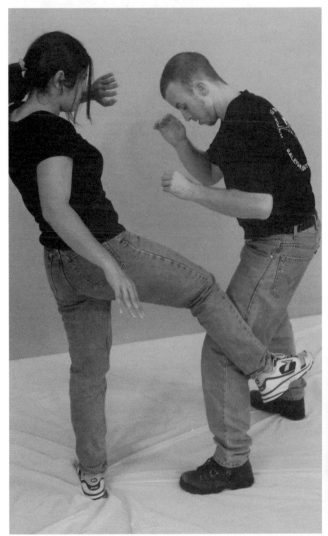

2. Hit with a fast low kick.

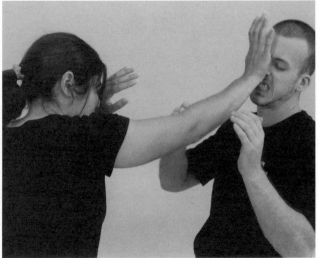

4. And finish with a right cross.

MUAY THAI KICKBOXING

Should you be knocked to the ground, this maneuver serves as a practical way of standing while defending yourself. Simply standing up would cause you to move closer to an attacker that is standing in front of you, but this move allows you to stand without moving closer to an opponent and ends with you in a fighting position.

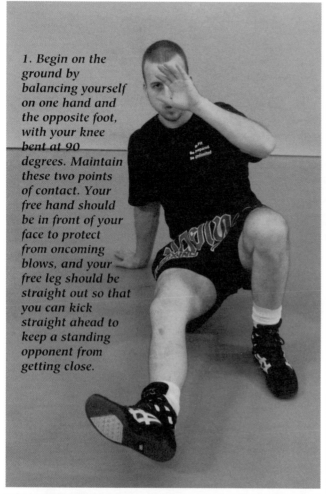

1. Begin on the ground by balancing yourself on one hand and the opposite foot, with your knee bent at 90 degrees. Maintain these two points of contact. Your free hand should be in front of your face to protect from oncoming blows, and your free leg should be straight out so that you can kick straight ahead to keep a standing opponent from getting close.

2. Next, quickly swing back on your grounded hand and come to your feet. This also creates distance between you and your adversary.

3. Continue to protect your face as you come to both feet.

4. Finish in a standing fighting position. Practice this move on both sides until you can do it quickly.

Basic Physical Conditioning

5

The following conditioning exercises use little or no equipment and can be done anywhere. Most of the exercises use your bodyweight as resistance to give the muscles a workout while getting the heart and lungs working. Any of these exercises can be used as a warm-up prior to a training session.

To track progress and intensity you can count repetitions or you can perform the exercises for a set amount of time. For example, you could jump rope for three minutes and immediately do 30 push-ups followed by two minutes of squat thrusts. You can make your Thai boxing workouts more demanding by doing these exercises in between rounds on the bag or pads. For example, doing squats or crunches during your one-minute rest between bag rounds would be a great way of getting some extra conditioning and pushing yourself a little more than usual.

After the general conditioning exercises we will detail several abdominal training exercises and routines. Strong abdominals aren't just for looks—they are the center of your body and must be strong enough to absorb blows in the ring. With proper conditioning you will be able to take shots to the belly that will amaze everyday civilians! Good, regular abdominal work and drills involving moderate abdominal toughening can make you as hard as a rock.

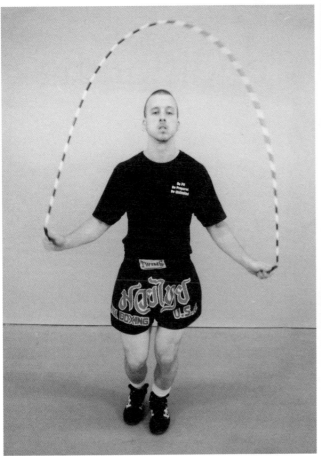

Jump rope: Keep your hands close to your body, elbows slightly bent. Use your wrists to swing the rope and only raise your feet (on the balls of your feet) a little off the floor just as the rope swings toward your toes. This is a great warm-up and also develops rhythm, timing, and hand-eye coordination.

Jumping jacks: Stand straight up with your feet together and your arms straight down at your sides. Bend your legs a little and jump slightly, simultaneously moving your arms upward until your hands touch each other above your head as your feet contact the floor. As you move your arms upward, spread your legs apart so that when you touch the floor again with your feet they are a little wider than shoulder width. Immediately jump back into the air again and return to the starting point.

Squats: Stand erect with your feet shoulder width apart, toes pointed slightly outward for balance, eyes fixed on a point straight ahead at eye level (keep focusing on this point throughout the lift). Keeping your torso erect, slowly bend your legs and lower yourself down into a squatting position. The tops of your thighs should not be lowered beyond a point parallel to the floor. Keep your head up and your hips out. To avoid stress upon the knee joint, do not let your knees extend over the end of your toes. Without bouncing, slowly straighten your legs and return to the standing position. To keep constant tension on the quadriceps, do not completely straighten your knees.

Jump squats: Stand erect with your feet shoulder width apart, toes pointed slightly outward for balance, eyes fixed on a point straight ahead at eye level (keep focusing on this point throughout the lift). Keeping your torso erect, slowly bend your legs and lower yourself down into a squatting position. The tops of your thighs should not be lowered beyond a point parallel to the floor. Keep your head up and your hips out. To avoid stress on the knee joint, do not let your knees extend over the end of your toes. Pause for a second and explode upward into a jump from the bottom of the squat. When you land, be sure to land with your knees bent.

Squat thrusts: Stand erect with your feet shoulder width apart, toes pointed slightly outside for balance, eyes fixed on a point straight ahead at eye level (keep focusing on this point throughout the move). Keeping the torso erect, slowly bend your legs and lower yourself down into a squatting position. The tops of your thighs should not be lowered beyond a point parallel to the floor. Keep your head up and your hips out. To avoid stress upon the knee joint, do not let your knees extend over the end of your toes. From the squat, place your hands on the floor in front of you and quickly straighten and extend your legs straight back. Without pausing, quickly return to the standing position and repeat. To make the exercise more difficult, add a jump at the end of each squat thrust, as shown previously.

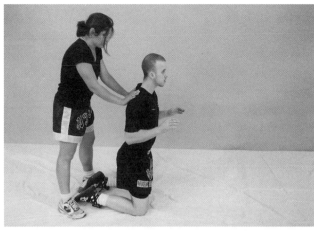

Hop between cones (both feet): Set up a pair of plyometric cones side by side and 2 to 3 feet apart. Begin with your left foot forward and hands up in a basic fighting stance. With your knees slightly bent, hop from side to side on the balls of your feet, building intensity and speed as you go. Periodically switch to performing this exercise on one foot and switch to the other foot and back to both.

Plyometric push-ups: Beginning with your knees bent, have a partner positioned behind you gently push you down. Roll forward on your knees and relax until you are just above the floor. Explode into the push-up just after stopping your downward momentum, then push hard enough to drive your torso all the way back up. Repeat.

Push-ups: Support your body weight on straight arms, contract your abs throughout the exercise, and keep your back straight. Bend your arms at the elbows until your chest is just above the floor. Slowly straighten your arms and push yourself to straight arm's length and repeat.

Medicine ball toss with partner: Face your partner and step directly backward about 5 feet each. One partner squats with the medicine ball held at chest level, elbows in and arms bent. Explode upward as you throw the ball upward and to your partner. Your partner catches the ball, landing in the squat position, and quickly repeats the exercise, keeping the tempo up.

Ground lunges: Begin on all fours, hips down and arms straight. Straighten one leg and bend the other knee up to your chest. Then straighten the bent leg and bring the opposite knee to your chest. Switch back and forth like this with speed, keeping your back straight and your weight supported on your hands.

Floor hyperextensions: Lie face down with limbs extended. Raise your straight legs and arms off the floor slowly. Lower and repeat.

Leg swings: While standing, balance on one leg and swing the other upward 5 to 10 times. Repeat on the other leg.

Shadowboxing: Shadowboxing is a way of practicing footwork, balance, and striking combinations, and increasing the heart rate. Move as if you were sparring with an opponent. Block, counterpunch, and keep your focus and intensity up. Practice pivoting, blocking, punching, kneeing, kicking, and elbowing an imaginary opponent. Your focus and intensity will determine the effectiveness of this exercise. A good routine is to do three- and four-punch combinations followed by a knee or kick, then a squat thrust. Move around a bit and repeat for the round, building the intensity each round for several short (two-minute) rounds.

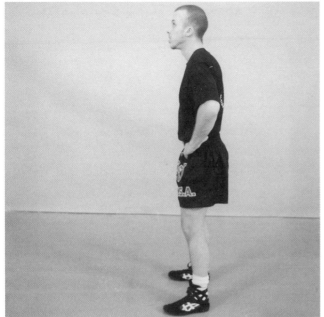

Walking lunges: Begin at one side of the floor, hands on your hips, feet about a foot apart, facing straight ahead. Take a long step forward with one foot and bend that knee deeply until it is at 90 degrees. Let the back leg bend also until the knee lightly touches the floor; keep the back straight. Straighten the bent leg and stand with the feet together again. With no rest, repeat with the other leg and continue the length of the floor and back. To make this more difficult, add light hand weights or do squats/jump squats on each end of the floor.

Circular footwork: Set up cones in a wide circle. As fast as you can, step either right or left and quickly move around the cones for agility, balance, conditioning, and the development of fast lateral footwork. Imagine there is an opponent in the center of the cones; keep your hips square, left foot forward, and hands up.

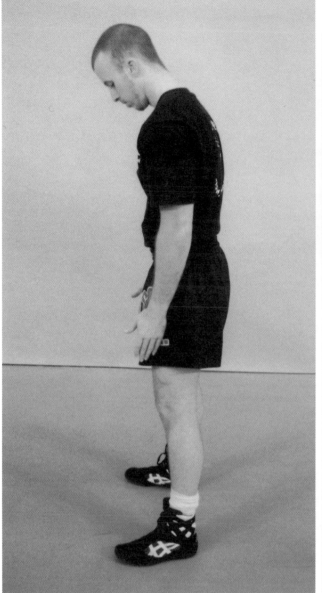

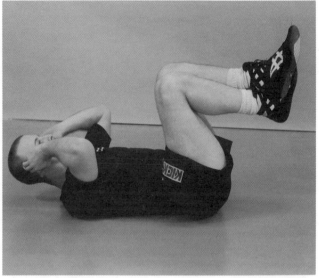

Neck rolls: Roll your head around slowly to loosen up the muscles of the neck. Raise and lower your chin and turn your head from side to side. This is an important warm-up prior to clench work or sparring.

Jogging: For a great warm-up or workout, jog outside or on a treadmill. Jog lightly, increasing your distance over time. This type of aerobic conditioning is discussed in detail in Chapter 8.

Crunches: Lie on your back and bend your knees at a 90-degree angle, thighs perpendicular to the floor. Either cross your arms across your chest or support the back of your head with your hands. Roll your shoulders toward your hips, slightly raising your hips off the floor and toward your shoulders. Breathe out. Hold momentarily and repeat.

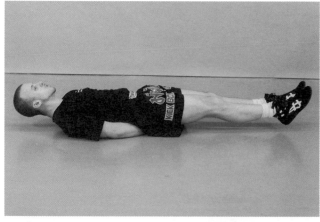

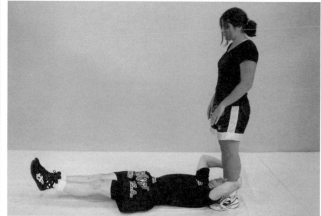

Stiff leg raises. Lie flat and place your hands under your hips. Extend your legs, keeping them a few inches off the floor (bend your knees slightly to prevent undue lower-back strain). Use abdominal strength to raise your legs in a semicircular arc to a point directly above your hips. Slowly lower your legs and repeat.

Leg rippers: Lie on your back, legs straight out. Have a training partner stand behind your head and get a tight grip on his/her ankles for support. Lift your feet three or four inches off the floor and keep them off the floor for the duration of the exercise. Forcefully swing your legs (knees just slightly bent) straight up to your partner's chest. Have your partner push your legs back down without letting them touch the floor. Repeat.

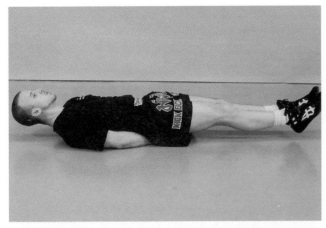

Knee ups: Lie flat and place your hands under your hips. Extend your legs, keeping them a few inches off the floor (bend your knees slightly to prevent undue lower-back strain). Bend your knees and bring them toward your face, rolling your hips at the top. Then straighten your legs again, keeping your feet a few inches off the floor.

Flutter kicks: Lie on your back with your hands under your hips, knees slightly bent, keeping your legs a few inches off the floor (parallel with your hips). Raise one leg straight up, and as you lower it back to the starting position lift the opposite leg. Repeat.

 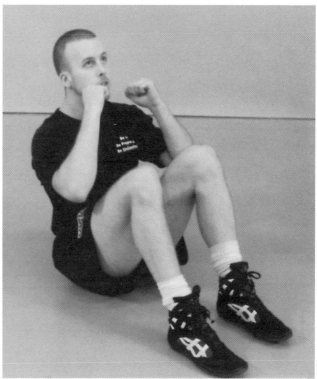

Sit-ups: Bend your knees and keep your feet on the floor, positioned under something sturdy or held down by a training partner. Keep your hands up and elbows bent. Bring your torso upward toward your knees, pause at the top of the exercise, and rotate to the left and the right, throwing left and right straight punches (1-2). Lower yourself back down and repeat.

Mid-range isometric sit-up.

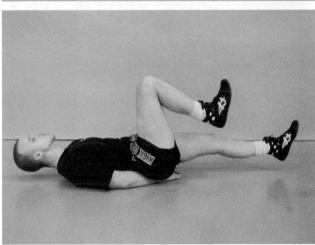

Two-count sit-ups (isometrics): Bend your knees and keep your feet on the floor, positioned under something sturdy or held down by a training partner. Keep your hands up and your elbows bent. Bring your torso upward toward your knees; pause at the halfway point, lift your chin, straighten your back, and stick your chest out. Hold this isometric abdominal contraction for 5 to 15 seconds (start with less time and increase by one or two seconds each repetition). Then complete the sit-up, going all the way up and then down slowly. Pause for a few seconds and repeat.

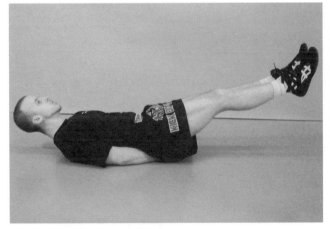

Bicycle kicks: Lie on your back with your hands under your hips, knees slightly bent. Keep your legs a few inches off the floor (parallel with your hips). Raise one knee so that it is bent at a 90-degree angle and raise the other leg so it is straight and parallel with the floor. Alternate positions, developing a rhythmic "peddling" motion similar to the leg movements used in peddling a bicycle.

Isometric stiff leg raises: Lie flat and place your hands under your hips. Extend your legs, keeping them a few inches off the floor. To prevent undue lower-back strain, bend the knees slightly. Use abdominal strength to raise your legs in a semicircular arc to a point directly above your hips. Slowly lower your legs and hold the middle position halfway down for 5-15 seconds. Repeat.

Roman chair crunches: Sit on the Roman chair with your instep under the footpad rollers and position your hips as comfortably as possible on the padded seat. Lean backward until your torso is at approximately a 30-degree angle with the floor. Sit forward enough to feel tension in the abdominal muscles, then rock slowly back into the low position and repeat the exercise in this short range of motion for the desired number of repetitions or seconds. You can add resistance by holding a weight plate or medicine ball during the exercise.

Medicine ball sit-ups: Get in a sit-up position and hold a medicine ball to your chest while a training partner stands on your feet. Concentrate on using abdominal strength as you curl your torso upward. When you reach the top, pass the ball to your partner and wait while he/she passes the ball back. Lower yourself with the medicine ball and repeat.

Folds: Begin by lying on your back with your legs straight and elbows bent, hands at your ears, head up. Simultaneously bend your knees, rolling the hips at the top, and curl your torso toward your knees. As you lower your torso, straighten your legs again (not letting your feet touch the ground). Repeat.

Medicine ball slams: Keep your hands up as your partner drives the medicine ball into your abdomen, simulating a body punch. To do this exercise correctly, keep the medicine ball close to the body, as shown, and use hip rotation to drive the ball into your partner's abdominal wall. Do not strike too high or you will hit the short ribs. Be sure to let your partner know how hard or light to do this. Begin by lightly touching the exposed abs and work your way to taking harder shots. This exercise is a must for fighters.

Jackknives: Lie on your back with your arms extended overhead along the floor. Bend your legs slightly to take potentially harmful stress off your lower back. Lift your torso and legs off the floor to bring them into a "V" with only your butt in contact with the floor. Lower and repeat.

Twists: Lie on your back on the training floor with your legs straight, knees slightly bent, feet off the floor a few inches, and hands beside your head. Bend one knee and raise your torso, twisting it enough so that you touch your raised knee with your opposite elbow. Lower and repeat on the opposite side.

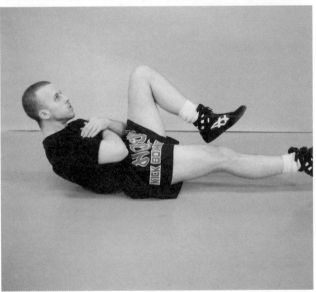

Isometric crunches: Lie on your back and bend one knee 90 degrees, thigh perpendicular to the floor, keeping the other leg straight (slight bend in the knee) and off the floor three to four inches. Either cross your arms over your chest or support the back of your head with your hands. Roll your shoulders toward your hips. Hold momentarily and repeat the exercise on both sides.

Hip ups: Lie on your back with your legs straight up in the air. Lift your hips off the floor so that your feet go up straight with the knees slightly bent. Lower and repeat.

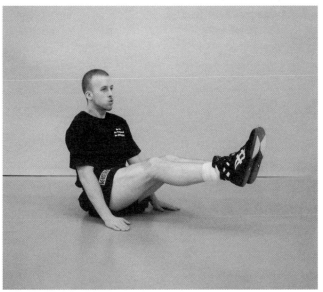

Heel taps: Sit on the floor with your legs straight in front of you. Brace yourself by placing your hands flat on the floor beside your upper legs. Slowly lift your feet straight up off the floor and hold for a second, then lower and repeat.

Reverse crunches: Lie on your back, legs bent at a 90-degree angle and your arms straight up. Lift your arms upward by raising only your shoulder blades off the floor, pause for a second, then lower and repeat.

CONDITIONING ROUTINES

Work the exercises for 30-second to one-minute rounds with minimal rest in between rounds. These exercises can serve as a warm-up before training in the gym. If you can't make it to the gym, simply work a group of exercises (approximately two and a half to five minutes total), stretch for two minutes, and go to the next list.

These are sample routines. Any exercises can be substituted using the five one-minute-round format.

- Jump rope
- Squat thrusts
- Push-ups (sets of 10)
- Medicine ball sit-ups
- Folds

- Crunches
- Squats
- Medicine ball tosses
- Isometric crunches (left side)
- Isometric crunches (right side)

- Squats
- Jump rope
- Floor lunges
- Jump squats
- Lunges

- Lunges
- Squats
- Lunges
- Jump squats
- Lunges

- Push-ups (10 count)
- Leg rippers
- Squat thrusts
- Shadowboxing
- Medicine ball tosses

- Jump rope
- Shadowboxing
- Push-ups
- Squats
- Crunches

CHAPTER 6

Weight Training Basics

The only way to improve your combat skills is by direct practice, which includes sparring and pad work. However, all other things being equal, the stronger athlete will prevail in a fight or any other athletic competition.

In the dark ages, coaches were afraid of recommending weight training for fear of slowing their athletes down. In the past several years, however, weight training has been accepted as a powerful training supplement for athletes in nearly every sport. One early example is Britain's Randy Turpin, who credited weight training as a powerful aid in winning the world boxing championship.[1] And look at today's athletes competing in Ultimate Fighting, boxing, and K-1 competitions: Their musculature could rival that of some bodybuilders. Of course, our purpose is not bodybuilding—you don't want to get knocked to the canvas because you spent too much time in the weight room and not enough time training for the fight.

If you are a competitive fighter, your goal will be to increase your strength as much as possible while staying in your desired weight class. Stronger muscles, tendons, and ligaments are less likely to be injured in training and competition. In addition, well-trained muscles have increased contractibility and will respond more readily to sudden exertion and explosive effort. Make no mistake—long-term weight training will not improve basic Thai-boxing skills, but it can enable the athletic skills to be used in a more efficient manner. Some additional benefits of regular weight training include:

- Improved athletic performance
- Stress relief
- Muscular growth
- Physical strength
- Fat loss
- Increased bone density

It is important to note that with increased muscle size also comes fat loss. Muscle is living tissue, which must burn calories (heat) to survive. With increased muscle tissue the body's metabolism increases drastically and more calories are burned all day, even while resting.[2]

Weight training also increases bone density and improves circulation. The body becomes more efficient when performing everyday activities.

Some swear by specialized machines, miracle protein supplements, or fad diets. More likely than not they have an ulterior motive for their bias. It is best to educate yourself as to how your body works and responds to training and diet. No miracle pill exists that will replace or duplicate hard work in the gym.

You should learn the basic weight-training exercises with a knowledgeable coach, starting slowly with relatively light weights. Study with a personal trainer who is skilled in demonstrating proper weight-training methods, such as one certified by the American Council on Exercise or the National Strength Conditioning Association.

But even though strength increases quickly as you begin routinely weight lifting, many people want miraculous, instant results and become discouraged. Remember that weight training is a discipline like Muay Thai; it requires some patience but brings tremendous results. Your motor skills will increase with experience, and you will gradually increase the amount of weight you can lift.

Finally, it is highly recommended that you train with a partner or spotter. A spotter is there to ensure your safety so that you are not crushed if you can't make a lift. A partner also will bring out your best by motivating you when you feel lazy and providing a little competition. If you must train alone, you should at least lift in a power rack. A rack (shown in the bench press and squat illustrations) has bars that will stop falling weights in case you miss a bench press. Two or three hundred pounds crashing down on your sternum is not an experience you will likely live to tell about.

PROGRESSIVE OVERLOAD

The otherwise healthy body adapts to resistance training by becoming stronger, increasing the thickness of muscle tissue, and becoming more coordinated. This is known as the overload principal, and it has been understood in one way or another since the days of ancient Greece. The overload principal applies no matter what type of equipment you use. As your muscles adapt to the weights, you will be able to do more reps with that weight than you could when you started. That is the time to add a little more weight to the bar and work your repetitions back up.

REPETITIONS

A *repetition* (rep) is the single performance of a given exercise. A *set* is a group of repetitions. For example, if someone performs a deadlift 10 times with 100 pounds, rests for one minute, and then repeats the exercise, he has done two sets of 10 repetitions. The rep ranges will be determined by your health and goals. A range of one to three repetitions is very low and allows for the use of maximum weights. Low-rep, heavy-weight training can only be done for short periods of time, as the stress to the joints should not be prolonged more than a few weeks. This type of training is used for developing raw power and strength. Moderate repetitions in the four-to-seven range are used for building strength as well as muscle size and thickness. Medium repetitions in the eight-to-12 range are great for general training as they increase strength, muscle size, muscle endurance, and are easier on the joints than using superheavy weights. Lastly, high repetitions of 12 to 20 using moderate weights are great for improving muscular endurance, a must for most competitive athletes.

This chart illustrates the percentage of one-repetition maximum, and rep ranges appropriate for various results in weight training.

Range	Reps	Weight	Percent of Maximum	Results
Low	1-3	Maximum	90-100 percent	Raw power and strength
Moderate	4-7	Heavy	80-90 percent	Strength, power, and size
Medium	8-12	Moderate	70-85 percent	Size, strength, and endurance
High	12-20	Light to moderate	>70 percent	Muscle endurance

EXERCISE PERFORMANCE

Each lifting exercise should first be performed slowly and through the full range of motion using relatively light weights. The range of motion is the number of degrees that a joint will move. The upward lifting portion of an exercise is the positive (concentric) part of the lift. Lowering the weight is the negative (eccentric) part of the lift. It is important to lower the weight under complete control.[3]

There are two basic methods of performing weight-training exercises, and they apply to both free weights and machines. The two methods are ballistic and rhythmic. The difference between the two methods lies in the performance of the positive portion of the exercise.

Ballistic training simply means that after lowering the weight (under control), you quickly and explosively drive the weight up. It is still important to maintain proper technique while lifting in a ballistic manner; that is, making sure that only the joints that are supposed to be involved in the lift are used. It is easy to swing the body, recruiting other muscles and generating momentum to assist you in bringing the weight up. But if your goal is to safely develop and train your muscles, then this practice will be detrimental to your progress. Cheating in this manner will give you the ego boost of lifting bigger weights but is not worth the risk of injury in the long term (just ask any ex-athlete suffering from crippling joint pain).

Ballistic training is usually done when training compound lifts, which is an exercise that makes many surrounding muscle groups work together to complete the lift (employing muscle synergy). For example, the squat is a compound lift that uses the quadriceps, lower back, trapezius, and hamstrings, while leg extensions are isolation exercises that work the quadriceps alone.

The other method of exercise performance is rhythmic lifting, which is used mainly for isolation exercises, although it is appropriate for compound exercises also. When lifting the weight (positive or concentric), one uses a slow, deliberate lifting motion. For example, when doing biceps curls, a count of two seconds up

three seconds down is appropriate. The rhythmic training is considered a safer method, as both positive and negative portions are done with complete control.

SETS AND PROGRESSION

The appropriate exercise selection, number of sets/repetitions, and exercise intensity varies with the individual. Determining factors include goals, age, experience, and health considerations. The weight-training progression means that if one week you can lift a weight, say 100 pounds for 10 reps, at the next session you should work for 11 to 12 reps. Once you can complete 12 reps without great effort, you should increase the weight slightly and drop back to 10 reps. This is how you grow stronger over a period of time; small increases in reps and weight add up to great results in a year or so.

It is beneficial to maintain a training log to note exercises, amounts of weight used, sets, and repetitions performed. The journal will give you a realistic look at your strength increases over time and is the best way of determining the appropriate weights for your current training cycle. Taking a look at the progress you have made over the weeks and months can be a great motivator. Also jot down the date and time of the workout and any other factors that you feel contribute to your physical performance, such as cardio work, stress, diet changes, or work schedules.

When beginning a weight-training program, it is best to work on an abbreviated routine using straight sets. An abbreviated routine is a weight-training session that includes one major exercise per muscle group, which means the entire body is trained during the workout. Straight sets are, as described earlier, one group of repetitions on a particular exercise. For those who are supplementing kickboxing or boxing with weight training, it is recommended that you warm up and cool down with three two-minute rounds of shadowboxing before and after each weight-training session. The rounds that you do after weight training will feel different because of the pumped-up, tight feeling that you will have in your muscles. Shadowboxing will serve to loosen up the muscles and keep you in the groove of striking, and the blood flow throughout the body will help reduce the next-day soreness.

In the next section I will go over some basic and advanced weight-training methods. The advanced methods are good for getting out of a "rut," or plateau, when you have become bored with the basic routine and your body is no longer responding. The advanced training methods are not necessary or suitable for beginner or intermediate athletes.

BASIC TRAINING METHODS

Pyramiding

Pyramiding is a safe and effective training method. The natural progression from lighter weights to heavier weights creates a built-in warm-up specific to the exercise. Begin an exercise with a relatively light weight and perform around 15 repetitions. After a one-minute rest, increase the weight enough so that you can do 10 to 12 reps. Again, rest 60 to 90 seconds and increase the weight again, this time selecting a weight that allows seven to 10 reps with some effort. Lastly, after 90 to 120 seconds' rest, select a heavier weight that you can lift in good form four to six times. Some athletes also perform a final "burnout" set of high repetitions with light weights to end the pyramid.

Sample weight	Repetitions	Rest time
50 lbs.	15	60 seconds
80 lbs.	12	90 seconds
100 lbs.	10	120 seconds
150 lbs.	6-8	2-4 minutes
180 lbs.	4-6	Done

Circuits

Circuit training is appropriate for muscular endurance training, but it does not allow the necessary rest time required for heavy weights. Set up an exercise station with the moderate weights preset on the weight machines or bars. The weight should allow 10 to 12 reps with some effort. One basic exercise station should be set up to work each muscle group: legs, back, chest, shoulders, arms, and abs.

Move from one exercise to the next with minimal rest time. After completing one set of each exercise with no rest between stations, allow yourself a normal rest period and repeat the circuit two more times for a total of three.

This method of training is great for cardiovascular conditioning, muscular strength, and endurance, and does not require a lot of time—usually a half-hour or less.

Periodization

This is a way of developing a long-term training plan that addresses different methods of training. Periodization calls for planning about four weeks of basic weight-training exercises using moderate weights for one set of eight to 15 reps. Over the next four to six weeks you increase the weight and perform lower repetitions (in the six-to-eight range) for multiple sets (two to five). In the third phase you go for all-out power, lifting heavy weights for low repetitions (one to five) and with plenty of rest time in between sets. After the power training, plan a few weeks of multiple-set, high-repetition training (eight to 15) with lower weights to improve muscular endurance.

This type of program will help keep you from getting bored because you change the program relatively often. Also, you will see tremendous results with less risk of injury because the program prepares you for the periods of heavy weightlifting by building up slowly.

ADVANCED TRAINING METHODS

Drop Sets

After a thorough warm-up, lift a moderate to heavy weight as many times as possible. Without resting, have your lifting partner decrease the weight by around 25 percent and continue the exercise, lifting the lighter weight as many times as possible. Follow this up with another immediate weight decrease of 25 percent and continue in the same manner until you are down to only 1/4th of your initial poundage. It is important to have a spotter with you in case you fail on a rep, and to change the weights for you to make the rest interval as short as possible. Any weight decrease can be used in this system; poundage can be dropped at 30, 20, or 10 percent to change the intensity. Remember, the lighter the drops, the more total repetitions are required.

With dumbbells, go "down the rack" with the weights. For example, after a warm-up, choose a dumbbell exercise, such as lateral raises for the shoulders, and perform a drop set starting with a fairly heavy weight (one you can manage for six to eight reps). Immediately grab the next set of weights 5 pounds lighter and get as many reps as you can, and so on until you are using the lightest dumbbells on the rack.

Supersets

A superset is a group of two exercises done one right after the other with no rest period in between and followed by a normal rest period. You can select two exercises for antagonistic muscle groups (chest/back, biceps/triceps, quadriceps/hamstrings), or you can use two exercises for the same muscle group (bench press/dumbbell flys, squats/leg extensions) for the superset. Trisets are a variation in which three straight exercises are done with a short rest afterward. A good example would be lateral raises, seated dumbbell presses, and rear laterals to work all three heads of the shoulder (deltoid) in succession.

Giant Sets

Giant sets are four to six exercises strung together in sequence followed by a normal rest period. The exercises can be for the same specific muscle or for surrounding muscle groups. For example, you could work leg extensions, squats, and lunges back to back to exhaust the quadriceps, immediately followed by leg curls and stiff-leg deadlifts to work all of the upper leg and hip muscles together. It is best to try this method after a few days of rest when you have no lingering muscle soreness.

Pre-exhaustion

With many compound exercises, the main muscle group that is utilized relies on the synergy of other muscles to complete the lift, forcing the weaker links to sometimes give out before maximizing the larger core muscles. For example, the bench press causes the large chest muscles (pectorals) to rely on the strength of the shoulders and triceps. Pre-exhaustion overcomes this problem by fatiguing the target muscle group with an isolation exercise before moving directly to the compound lift. For the example given earlier, a set of moderate dumbbell flys done before each set of bench presses would prefatigue the chest muscles, increasing the effectiveness of the bench work on those muscles.

Peak Contraction

This training approach puts maximal stress on target muscles by utilizing isometric muscle contraction. Isometric muscle contraction differs from concentric and eccentric in that there is no actual movement of the joint. For example, holding the bottom position of a squat will cause an isometric contraction of the affected muscles. This principal is useful in weight-training exercises such as the barbell curl, because when the arms are fully bent at the top of the movement, the weight is actually being supported by the deltoids, not the targeted biceps. By holding the weight when the elbows are flexed at 90 degrees, you are placing great stress on the biceps. Try holding the peak-contracted position for five to 10 seconds on the last repetition of an exercise to feel the effects.

Continuous Tension

Continuous tension is achieved by moving the weight about half as fast as normal on a given exercise, concentrating fully on "squeezing" the targeted muscles. After the targeted number of full-range reps has been completed, finish up with three or four burnout reps. (These are reps done at regular speed but only through half the normal range of motion.)

Superslow Repetitions

Simply perform all repetitions in your routine extremely slowly. Try to take a total of 14 seconds per rep for each set, lowering the weight for seven seconds and lifting it for seven seconds. Reps will be lower than usual; around six to eight is appropriate. This type of training recruits maximal muscle fibers and causes tremendous results in muscle size and endurance. This type of exercise can be hard to endure but is well worth the effort. Remember to decrease your weight training frequency and duration with this training method, spending no more than 20 minutes on the weights once per week per muscle group.

Negative Reps

Exercise physiologists acknowledge that the lowering (eccentric) portion of an exercise is the most stressful and effective to the muscles. Negative reps require a spotter to raise the weights, which you then lower as slowly as you can two to four times. This training is extremely stressful on the body and should not be done for prolonged periods; only a few workouts will produce strength gains.

Rest/Pause

Another method of power building is the rest/pause technique. Your body recovers a great deal in a short period of time during anaerobic training. While full recovery may take a minute or so, your body will recover roughly 50 percent of its strength and endurance in 15 to 20 seconds. Therefore after a maximum effort set using heavy weight, you can take a brief 15-second rest/pause and go right back to the exercise for an additional one to three repetitions. For best results, this kind of power training should be used sparingly and with caution. Burnout can happen quickly with hard training, especially when coupled with the demands of other physical activities.

OVERTRAINING

Overtraining—whether it's a result of strenuous weight training, cardiovascular work, martial arts training, or outside mental and physical stresses—can wreak havoc, not only on your training progress, but also your health. You need to factor in a few weeks a year for total rest to relax and recharge your batteries. Training in the martial arts and cross-training conditioning should be fun as well as rewarding. Your body's energy systems are like a bank account: You can only make "withdrawals" if you have made significant "deposits." Ample sleep, good food, rest, and relaxation are the necessary "deposits."

Overtraining can often be blamed on too many lengthy workouts per week rather than the intensity level of the individual workouts. You can work hard or you can work long, but you cannot do both simultaneously. The three variables involved in athletic training are represented in the fitness equation F.I.T., which stands for frequency, intensity, and time.

- *Frequency.* How many workouts do you perform per week? This includes weights, kickboxing, and running.
- *Intensity.* How difficult are your training sessions? A scale of one to 10 can be used to gauge the intensity.
- *Time.* How long does a workout last? The more intense the workout, the less time it should take.

The three factors must be balanced for productive training. Too many workouts per week for an extended period can wear the body down beyond its capacity to rebuild and repair itself, leading to illness or injury. If you display more than one of the following symptoms, it is likely that you are in an overtrained state:

- Lethargy, constant fatigue
- Persistently sore joints and/or muscles
- Loss of appetite
- Insomnia
- Illness and/or chronic infections
- Lack of enthusiasm
- High morning pulse rate
- Elevated blood pressure not caused by other factors
- Irritability/unusually short temper

An ounce of prevention is worth a pound of cure. Don't confuse sufficient rest with laziness. If you feel overtraining is affecting you, take one or two weeks off and be sure to get plenty of healthy food and sleep to refuel the body.

MINOR INJURY TREATMENT

Every athlete experiences various minor injuries at one time or another. Pain goes with the territory, especially in combat sports like Muay Thai (you don't have to be a masochist to enjoy the sport, but it helps). For most minor sports-related injuries you should remember the acronym *RICE*: rest, ice, compression, and elevation. Usually this treatment is best used for

RICE

Rest: Lay off activities that aggravate the injured area. This can mean the difference between a fast recovery and a nagging injury that persists for months. Better to take a few days or a week off and not try to work through it.

Ice: Ice reduces the blood flow to the injured area, which deadens the nerves and decreases the feeling of pain. Ice also reduces swelling. Apply the ice pack to the affected area for no more than 15 to 20 minutes at a time. Ice can be applied numerous times a day for the duration of an injury. Put a cloth between the ice and your skin, as ice burns (frostbite) can occur if you apply the ice directly with no barrier.

Compression: Another way to reduce swelling is to put pressure on the swollen area. Wrapping an Ace bandage snugly around the area will do the trick. Special wraps are available for the knee, wrist, elbow, and ankle joints, also.

Elevation: Waste products and fluids accumulate around injured areas and can be drained by elevating an injured limb. I have seen guys whose ankles swelled up like baseballs from the blood and fluid that drained from their bruised shins. Elevation, in conjunction with the other RICE treatments, can provide effective relief and recovery.

two days following a minor injury. Of course, you need to use your judgment, as some injuries are serious and require a doctor's care (like when you see a bone protruding through the skin). If you feel you need to be looked at by a doctor, do not hesitate to see one.

Heat

Heat is, in some cases, a better injury treatment than ice. In the case of muscle cramps, stiffness, or soreness from taking leg kicks in sparring or from heavy weight training, heat is the best alternative. When you are training and taking lots of kicks to the legs, scar tissue and waste products can build up, causing stiffness and pain. Heat will increase the blood flow to that area, bringing more nutrients to the tissue and flushing out waste products. Do not put the heat source directly on the skin unless you want to have some burns to go along with your injury; as with ice, have a cloth layer on top of your skin. After applying heat for 10 to 20 minutes, stretch the muscle gently and massage the area afterwards. Massaging the area will help with circulation of blood to the damaged muscle, and stretching will help it retain some strength and improve the range of motion.

Shin Splints

Most people who run experience shin splints, or pain in the front of the lower leg. In some cases the shin muscles can actually separate from the bone at the tendon. Shin splints can be caused by several factors, including exercising more than your body is used to, unusual conditions (like running downhill for the first time), or wearing new shoes. If pain is crippling or severe, it is advisable to get your lower leg scanned by a doctor to rule out the possibility of a stress fracture. To help stop shin splints early, back off of running for a few days and start back gradually. Icing the shins will help reduce the swelling and reduce the pain by numbing the nerves. And if need be, your doctor can recommend an anti-inflammatory—a medicine that will help reduce swelling and inflammation.

To stretch the muscles around the shins

before and after training, use a wall as support and place one foot behind the other. Bend the front knee slightly and straighten the back leg with the top of the foot (toes) on the floor. Lean the hips forward. Hold the stretch for 15 to 20 seconds and repeat on the opposite leg. (See photo in Chapter 9.)

●●●

1. Kirkley, George. *Weight Lifting and Weight Training.* New York: Bell Publishing, 1973.
2. Cotton, Richard T. *Personal Trainer Manual,* San Diego, CA: American Council on Exercise, 1996.
3. ibid.

Weight Training Exercises and Programs

SQUATS

Squats exercise the quadriceps, buttocks, and lower-back muscles. Squats also stress the shoulder girdle, hamstrings, and abdominals (these muscles stabilize the body during exercise execution). These muscles are used in the push kick, exploding forward, ducking, striking with the knee, and lifting the leg to block low kicks.

How to: Squats are performed with free weights. Begin with a barbell supported across a squat or power rack, bend your legs and position the bar across your upper back and shoulder muscles. Pad the bar with a towel if desired. Grip the bar wider than shoulder width

to balance it across the upper back. Straighten your legs while keeping the upper back and abdominal muscles tight to lift the bar from the rack. Start the lift while standing erect with your feet shoulder width apart, toes pointed slightly outside for balance and eyes fixed on a point straight ahead at eye level (keep focusing on this point throughout the lift).

Keeping the torso erect, slowly bend your legs and lower yourself down into a squatting position. The tops of the thighs should not be lowered beyond a point parallel to the floor.

Keep the head up and the hips out. To avoid stress on the knee joint, do not let the knees extend over the end of your toes. Without bouncing, slowly straighten your legs and return to the standing position as illustrated. A weightlifting belt is recommended for stability and abdominal support. As with all lifting movements, consciously breathe out during the exertion phase of the lift and inhale during the "lowering" phase. Never hold your breath, as this could lead to unconsciousness or even death.[1]

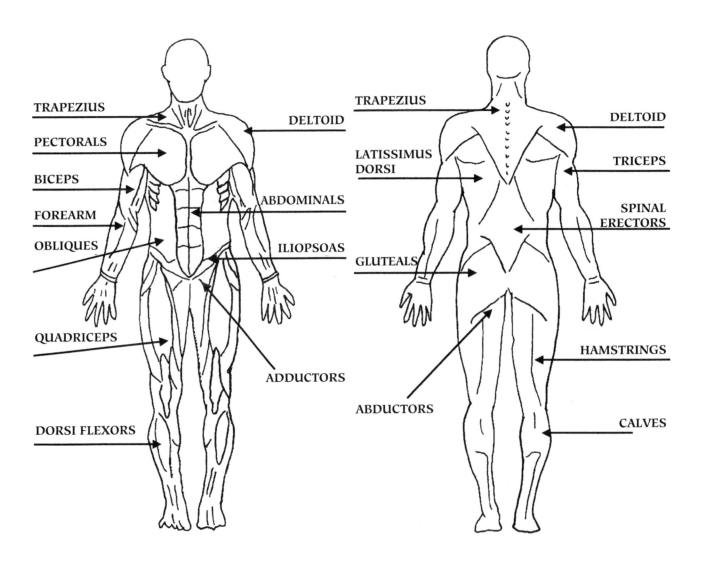

TRAPEZIUS
PECTORALS
BICEPS
FOREARM
OBLIQUES
QUADRICEPS
DORSI FLEXORS
DELTOID
ABDOMINALS
ILIOPSOAS
ADDUCTORS

TRAPEZIUS
LATISSIMUS DORSI
GLUTEALS
ABDUCTORS
DELTOID
TRICEPS
SPINAL ERECTORS
HAMSTRINGS
CALVES

LEG EXTENSIONS

The seated leg extension isolates the quadriceps almost completely. Little effort is needed by surrounding muscle groups to stabilize the body. The quadriceps are used with the hips in the push kick, in ducking, and exploding forward.

How to: Seat yourself on the weight machine with good posture and grasp the side handles of the machine. Keep your abdomen tight throughout the exercise. The roller pad should be on the insteps of your feet. Moving only your lower legs, smoothly straighten your legs until your knees are almost fully extended, keeping constant tension on the targeted muscles. Lower your legs slowly and repeat for the desired number of reps. This exercise can be performed with one leg at a time for extra isolation or knee rehabilitation.

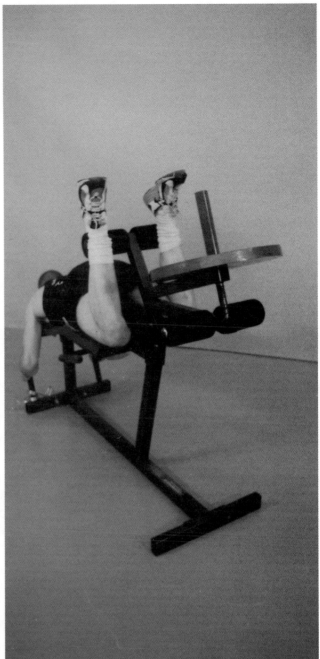

LEG CURLS

Lying leg curls isolate the muscles of the hamstrings located in the backs of the legs, with minimal involvement from surrounding muscle groups. The hamstrings are used in forward and backward movement as well as in executing the spinning back kick.

How to: Lie face down on the padded surface of the leg-curl machine with your knees at the edge of the pad toward the lever arm.

Hook the backs of your heels on the roller pad and completely straighten your legs and tighten your abdomen. Grasp the outside handles (if provided) to brace yourself. To keep from using the lower back to lift your hip structure, make sure your pelvis is always in contact with the pad. Slowly bend your knees as fully as you can, pausing at the top for one second or so. Slowly lower the legs and repeat for the desired number of reps.

STIFF-LEG DEADLIFTS

The stiff-leg deadlift is an excellent compound lift that puts stress upon the hamstrings, gluteus (buttocks), and muscles of the lumbar region of the lower back. It is very easy to add a shrug at the end of the lift to exercise the trapezius as well. The hamstrings are used in forward and backward movement as well as in executing the spinning back kick. The lower back is used with the neck (trapezius) muscles in keeping the body and head upright while fighting in the clench position, essential for avoiding a knee to the face.

How to: Stand with your shins touching the barbell or dumbbells placed on the floor. Bend and take a shoulder-width grip on the bar and stand erect, with your arms straight and at your sides, the bar resting on your upper thighs. Straighten your legs and keep them straight (hence the name stiff-leg deadlift!) through the lift. Slowly bend over at the waist, tilting the hips up and keeping the head up, until your torso is at 90 degrees to the floor. Slowly stand erect to complete the lift.

Since you are placing your lower back in a weakened position, begin with light weights and perform slowly and smoothly. As with all lifting movements, consciously breathe out during the exertion phase of the lift and inhale during the lowering phase. Never hold your breath, as this could lead to unconsciousness and death.

LUNGE

The lunge stresses the muscles of the quadriceps (especially the upper thigh area), gluteus, and upper hamstrings. The calves, upper back muscles, and the abdominals act as stabilizers during the lift. These muscles are used in the push kick, exploding forward, ducking, striking with the knee, and lifting the leg to block low kicks.

How to: Grasp a pair of dumbbells or barbells and hold them with your arms at your sides. Stand erect with your head up. Place your feet about shoulder width apart, toes pointed straight ahead. Step with one foot about 3 feet straight ahead, with the toes forward. Maintain a straight back and bend the back leg until the knee is nearly touching the floor. In this position you should feel a strong stretching sensation in the hip and quad area of the lead foot. Push off smoothly with your lead leg and return to the starting position. Repeat the exercise with the opposite leg for the next rep. Perform the desired number of reps for each leg.

TOE RAISE

The elevated toe raise isolates the muscles of the calf. These muscles are essential for staying on your toes while boxing and can generate extra power on the push kick and round kick as you transfer your body weight to the ball of your foot. Strong calves are necessary for execution of footwork when you are fatigued. Look at any successful fighter and you will see well-developed lower leg muscles.

How to: Begin with the balls of your feet on the end of a block or a stair step. Lower your heels toward the ground until you feel a significant (but not excessively painful) stretch in the calf muscles and Achilles tendon. Keeping a slight bend in the knees and an erect posture, lift your heels slowly in one smooth motion, raising yourself as high on your toes as is possible. Pause in the top position and repeat for the desired number of reps.

DEADLIFT

The deadlift works the lumbar region of the back, the quadriceps, hamstrings, calves, latissimus dorsi, upper back, and shoulder girdle muscles. The abdominal muscles also play a big role in stabilizing the entire body. The upper and lower leg muscles are used in forward and backward movement as well as in executing various kicks. The lower back is used with the neck (trapezius) muscles in keeping the body and head upright while fighting in the clench position, essential for avoiding a knee to the face. The lats generate power in hooking punches, and thick lats provide some protection for the ribs.

How to: Begin by standing close to a loaded barbell on the floor, and place your feet shoulder width apart. Bend at the legs and hips, taking a mixed grip (one hand over, one under) on the bar. Keep the head up and back flat with no rounding of the spine. Straighten your arms, flatten your back, and position yourself so that your hips are lower than your shoulders and your knees are lower than your hips. This is the best mechanical position for lifting anything off the floor. Begin the lift by straightening your legs and lifting from the quads and hips. Slowly stand erect, keeping your eyes focused on a point straight ahead, similar to when doing squats. Finish the lift with a shoulder shrug while standing erect (lift your shoulders toward your ears). Slowly lower yourself into the starting position, bending at the hips and knees. As with all lifting movements, consciously breathe out during the exertion phase of the lift and inhale during the lowering phase. Never hold your breath, as this could lead to unconsciousness and death.

CHINS

The chin puts heavy, strong stress on the latissimus dorsi, rear deltoids, biceps, and brachialis (forearm) muscles. Chins develop functional strength in the entire body as you must stabilize yourself throughout the exercise and keep your body from swinging. The lats generate power in hooking punches, and thick lats provide some protection for the ribs. The biceps and shoulders generate power in uppercuts and hooks.

How to: Jump to grasp the handles of an overhead chinning bar with your palms in, hands spaced about shoulder width apart. Begin with your arms straight and curl your legs behind you as shown. Keep the abdomen tight throughout the exercise. Concentrate on pulling your elbows down and back (elbows close in to the body) as you pull yourself up. Finish the exercise with the top of your chest touching the bar with your back slightly arched. Lower yourself slowly and repeat.

 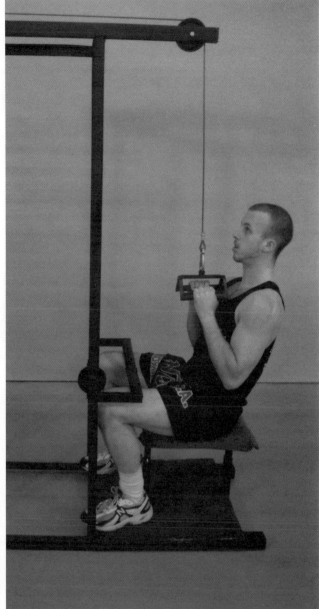

SEATED PULLDOWNS

The seated pulldown works the same basic muscle groups as the chin, lats, rear deltoids, biceps, and forearms; however, pulldowns require less synergistic effort from the body as a whole. This is a great exercise for individuals who have not yet developed the strength or body control to pull their own body weight. The lats generate power in hooking punches, and thick lats provide some protection for the ribs. The biceps and shoulders generate power in uppercuts and hooks.

How to: Various grips are available to stress your upper back muscles at different angles; the same basic movements still apply with concessions for varying grips. Have a seat at the pulley machine and place the tops of your thighs under the roller pads. Reach up and grip the bar, keeping the back straight and abdominals tight. Maintain this position throughout the exercise. Concentrate on pulling your elbows down and back (elbows close to the body) as you pull the bar down. Finish the exercise with the top of your chest touching the bar with your back slightly arched. Slowly control the weight on the way back up.

Pulldowns with a wide grip bar start.

Pulldowns with a wide grip bar finish.

SHRUGS

The shrug can be done with a barbell, dumbbells, or on a variety of machines. Emphasis is primarily placed upon the trapezius muscles of the upper shoulder girdle. Secondary emphasis is placed on the forearm flexors and deltoids. The trapezius muscles are responsible for powerful uppercuts and, as these muscles surround the neck, the development of them can help keep you from serious injury.

How to: Hold a barbell with straight arms; the bar should be lightly touching the thighs, with your knees slightly bent. Standing straight, tighten your abdomen. Keeping the arms straight, try to touch the tops of your shoulders to your ears. Hold the top position for a moment to fully contract the trapezius muscles. Lower and repeat for reps.

BENT-OVER ROWS

This is an excellent exercise for developing the upper back muscles. Primary stress is on the latissimus dorsi, rhomboids, posterior deltoid, biceps, brachialis, and forearm muscles. Some secondary emphasis is on the lower back muscles. The lats generate power in hooking punches, and thick lats provide some protection for the ribs. The biceps and shoulders generate power in uppercuts and hooks.

How to: Begin by placing your feet slightly beyond shoulder width about 2 feet from the bar. Bend over at the knees and hips and take a slightly wider than shoulder width overgrip on the bar. Do not fully straighten your knees during this lift; keep a bend in the knee. You want your torso parallel to the floor, arms hanging straight down with the weight a little off the floor. Keeping your torso motionless (no "swinging"), slowly bend your arms and pull the weight up until the bar touches your lower rib cage. The upper arms should move up at a 45-degree angle from your torso. Lower under control and repeat.

ONE-ARM BENT ROWS

This movement works the same muscles as the barbell variation but avoids any stress to the lower back—great for those with lower-back trouble. Primary stress is on the latissimus dorsi, rhomboids, posterior deltoid, biceps, brachialis, and forearm muscles. Some secondary emphasis is on the trapezius. The lats generate power in hooking punches, and thick lats provide some protection for the ribs. The biceps and shoulders generate power in uppercuts and hooks.

How to: With a dumbbell close to the side of a flat bench, position yourself so that one knee is bent and resting on the bench, with the opposite leg slightly bent, foot on the floor. Support yourself on the bench with the hand you will not be rowing with. Keeping your torso parallel to the floor, grasp the dumbbell and hold it with your arm straight, head up, looking forward. Keeping the elbow in, slowly bend your arm and pull the weight upward until it touches the side of your rib cage. Do not let your spine twist; keep your torso straight during the lift. Lower slowly and repeat.

POWER CLEANS

The power clean is a functional exercise that will develop explosive power, strength, anaerobic capacity, coordination, and body control. It synergistically works all the major muscle groups of the back, hips, legs, shoulder girdle, arms, and forearms. The lift takes some practice, and getting the help of a knowledgeable trainer is highly recommended. This exercise works every muscle used in every athletic activity except for the muscles of the chest. It also stimulates the metabolism and works the heart and lungs.

How to: Step up to a barbell on the gym floor with your shins lightly touching the bar, feet slightly past shoulder width. Reach down and take a shoulder-width overgrip on the bar. Keeping your arms straight and your back flat, squat down with your back at approximately 45 degrees to the floor, shoulders above your hips, and hips above the level of your knees.

Initiate the pull from the floor by straightening your legs. Follow up immediately with an extension of your torso, bringing it to a vertical position, and simultaneously whipping your elbows under the bar to fix it to your shoulders. Dip your body about 6 inches as you whip the bar to shoulder level.

If you are using moderate weights, follow through with an overhead military press. Avoid arching backward when pressing the weight, and keep your elbows in, abs tight, and eyes straight ahead.

Lower the weight back to the floor by reversing the instructions given for the upward phase of the lift. A lifting belt is highly recommended for this exercise. Also, you will have to eliminate the press portion when using heavy weights. As with all lifting movements, consciously breathe out during the exertion phase of the lift and inhale during the "lowering" phase. Never hold your breath, as this could lead to unconsciousness and death.

ROMAN CHAIR HYPEREXTENSIONS

This exercise effectively isolates the spinal erector, gluteus, and hamstring muscles. The hamstrings are used in forward and backward movement as well as in executing the spinning back kick. The lower back is used with the neck (trapezius) muscles in keeping the body and head upright while fighting in the clench position, essential for avoiding a knee to the face.

How to: Position yourself on the Roman chair so that you are face down, hips on the seat pad, with the backs of your ankles resting on the roller pads. Keep your legs straight, hands behind your head, and head up as you do the exercise. Flex your torso forward at the waist until your torso is vertical to the floor.

Raise your trunk upward and backward until your torso is in a position just above parallel to the floor. To avoid compression of the vertebrae, do not arch excessively. Return to the starting position and repeat slowly.

BENCH PRESS

The bench press strongly stresses the pectorals, anterior deltoids, and triceps. Secondary stress is on the latissimus dorsi and the medial deltoid. This is a good basic upper-body exercise, but one that is often overused. The chest, shoulders, and triceps are used in straight punches and in pushing away opponents.

How to: Lying on a flat bench, position your hands at an even distance apart about 3 to 4 inches beyond shoulder width. Place your feet on the floor for balance. Straighten your arms to bring the bar off the rack and rotate your shoulder blades in toward the bench. Support the weight directly above your shoulder joints.

Lower the weight by bending your arms slowly, staying in control. As you lower the weight, let it travel down toward your lower chest in a slight arc. Pause for a second either when the bar lightly touches your chest or when your arms are bent at a 90-degree angle. Keeping your butt on the bench, push the weight in a slight arc back to the starting position over the shoulders.

Violently arching your back and lifting your butt from the bench may give you an ego boost as it allows you to lift heavier weights; however, using this momentum will also give you pain in the lower back in the days to come. As with all lifting movements, consciously breathe out during the exertion phase of the lift and inhale during the lowering phase. Never hold your breath, as this could lead to unconsciousness and death.

INCLINE PRESS

The incline press with dumbbells or a barbell strongly works the upper pectorals, anterior deltoid, and triceps. Secondary stress is on the latissimus dorsi and the medial deltoid. The use of dumbbells requires more balancing, muscle control, and coordination than the barbell variation. The chest, shoulders, and triceps are used in straight punches and in pushing away from the body.

How to: Begin on an incline bench with your hips and upper back in contact with the pad, lower back slightly arched. Grip the bar with the palms forward and hold the weight over your collarbones with your arms straight.

Slowly bend your arms down, with your elbows down and back, until you feel a good stretch in the chest. Push the weights back to straight arm's length and repeat slowly for reps.

When using dumbbells, the weights can be pressed in two ways: the triangle or straight line. With the triangle, the weights touch at the top of the lift and are lowered wide at the bottom position to form a "triangle." The straight line presses the dumbbells in a straight line from top to bottom, just like using a bar.

INCLINE DUMBBELL CHEST FLYS

The incline fly works the same muscles as the incline dumbbell press (upper pectorals, anterior deltoids, medial deltoids) but stresses the pectoral muscles more effectively—and with less weight—than presses. (Flys, unlike presses, do not involve the triceps.) The chest, shoulders, and triceps are used in straight punches and in pushing away from the body.

How to: Begin by sitting on an incline bench while holding a pair of dumbbells and resting on your thighs, arms bent at 90 degrees. As you lie back on the incline, kick your knees up to help hoist the weights straight above you at arm's length. Situate yourself so that your hips and upper back are in contact with the pad, lower back slightly arched. Begin with your elbows rotated out and away from the body, arms straight above your chest. Slowly lower the dumbbells in a semicircular arc and simultaneously bend your elbows, "opening your arms" until you feel a stretch in the pectoral muscles. At this point your elbows should be below the level of your torso. Hold this position for a second, and then slowly bring the weights back up.

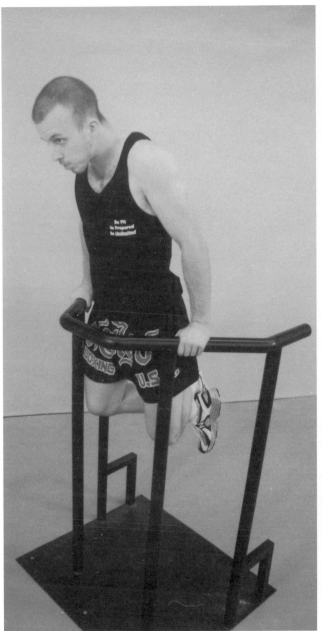
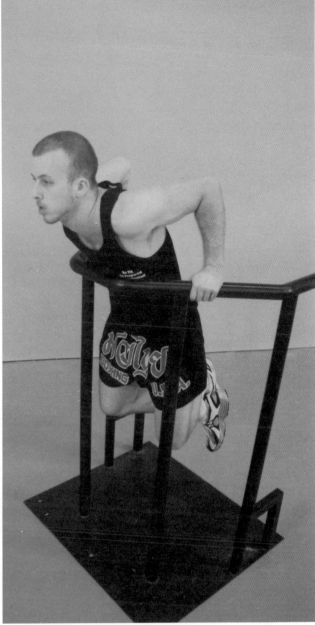

DIPS

The dip strongly stresses the pectorals, anterior deltoids, and triceps. Secondary stress is on the latissimus dorsi and the medial deltoid. Dips use your own body weight as resistance and, as such, are valuable in attaining body control, awareness, and synergistic coordination. The chest, shoulders, and triceps are used in straight punches and in pushing away from the body.

How to: Begin by hopping up into position with your arms straight and hands a few inches wider than shoulder width, evenly spaced. Keep your torso tilted slightly forward, legs crossed behind you.

Slowly bend your elbows—keeping the shoulder girdle stable—and lower yourself until your arms are bent at a 90-degree angle. Keeping your elbows closer to your body will stress your triceps more, and elbows out and away from the body shifts more stress to the chest and shoulders. Exhale and slowly straighten your arms, bringing you back to the top position.

SEATED DUMBBELL SHOULDER PRESS

The dumbbell press works the anterior and medial deltoid, as well as the triceps. Secondary stress is on the posterior deltoid and upper back muscles. The shoulders are vital in throwing any punch and can easily be damaged if not trained properly. The shoulders are involved in every movement of the upper arm.

How to: Clean a pair of dumbbells to your shoulders, rotating your palms so that they are facing forward. Slowly push the weights to arm's length overhead, then lower slowly. Repeat. As with the incline dumbbell press, you can press using a triangle or straight-line variation. To keep continuous tension on the shoulders, do not pause at the top of the exercise; instead, lower the weights just before you press them all the way up.

DUMBBELL LATERAL RAISES

The lateral raise exercises the medial deltoid and the trapezius. The shoulders are vital in throwing any punch and can easily be damaged if not trained properly. The shoulders are involved in every movement of the upper arm.

How to: Grab two dumbbells, place your feet shoulder width apart, and stand erect. Bend slightly forward at the waist and keep your palms facing each other at your sides. Keep your arms slightly rounded (or bent a little at the elbows) throughout the movement. Keeping your palms facing the floor, slowly raise the weights in a semicircular arc out to the side and slightly forward until they are a little above the level of your shoulders. Concentrate on lifting your elbows out and up during the exercise. Lower the weights and repeat.

DUMBBELL BENT LATERAL RAISE

This movement stresses the posterior deltoid along with the upper back muscles.

The shoulders are vital in throwing any punch and can easily be damaged if not trained properly. The shoulders are involved in every movement of the upper arm.

How to: Grab two light dumbbells. With your feet set shoulder width apart, bend your torso so that it is parallel to the floor. Hang your arms downward from your shoulders, palms facing inward, with the dumbbells touching each other. Slightly bend both arms and keep them rounded throughout.

Slowly raise the dumbbells in semicircular arcs directly out to the sides until they are above shoulder level. Concentrate on trying to touch your elbows together behind your back (this, by the way, is highly improbable barring some heinous genetic condition), and keep your elbows going toward your ears (away from the body). Lower the weights and repeat.

ROTATOR CUFF RAISE

This movement stresses the four muscles of the rotator cuff in the deltoid. These small but important muscles are the supraspinatus, infraspinatus, teres minor, and subscapularis. The rotator cuff muscles are often injured in heavy weight training and through overhand throwing movements such as punching (the overhand right) or throwing a baseball. This exercise can be therapeutic to an injured shoulder and serve to strengthen these specific muscles to avoid future injury.

How to: Hold a lightweight plate (no more than 5 pounds) or dumbbell in your hand with your arm bent at a 90-degree angle. With your forearm parallel to the floor and your palm down, slowly raise your hand so that your palm is facing forward. Lower slowly and repeat for an equal number of reps on both sides.

TRICEPS BENCH DIP

Triceps dips, when done correctly, stress the external and middle heads of the triceps, with some stress to the internal triceps head. The triceps extend the upper arm and are used in straight punches.

How to: Place your hands on a flat bench at shoulder width, fingers pointed toward your toes. Straighten your arms completely. Slowly bend your arms at the elbows as completely as possible, lowering your torso. Push your body up and away from the bench to complete the exercise.

TRICEPS PUSHDOWNS

The pushdown exercises the external head of the triceps with secondary emphasis on the middle and internal head of the muscle. The triceps extend the upper arm and are used in straight punches.

How to: Grab the triceps rope or straight bar. Set your feet slightly wider than shoulder-width apart and step back with one leg so that one foot is ahead of the other. Next, lean forward at the waist, angling your torso toward the weight stack. This position will help keep you from pushing forward with your body for assistance when your arms fatigue.

Keeping your elbows pinned to your sides, start the lift with your arms bent at a 90-degree angle, forearms parallel to the floor. Bending the elbows, slowly push the rope to straight arm's length; do not lock the elbows at the end. Control the weight as it travels slowly back up without momentum. Repeat for reps.

| LYING SKULL CRUSHERS | TRICEPS DUMBBELL KICKBACKS |

The skull crushers work the internal and middle heads of the triceps. The triceps extend the upper arm and are used in straight punches.

How to: Take an overgrip on the middle of the bar with about 6 inches between your hands. Lie face up on the bench with your feet planted on the floor for balance, and extend your arms straight above your shoulders.

Keeping your elbows forward, and without moving your upper arms, slowly bend your elbows, lowering the bar in a semicircular arc from the starting position down to your forehead. Concentrate on contracting the triceps as you slowly push the weight back along the same arc to the starting position.

The kickback is a great exercise for isolating the triceps, particularly the outer and medial triceps. The triceps extend the upper arm and are used in straight punches.

How to: Grip a light dumbbell in your left hand with your palm toward your body for the entire movement. Rest your right knee and right palm on the bench to steady yourself, your torso parallel to the floor. Pin your left arm, which should be bent at 90 degrees, into the side of your torso, upper arm parallel to the floor.

Slowly straighten your left arm. Allowing no shoulder movement, hold the weight at straight arm's length for a second and lower the weight back to the starting position. Repeat with both arms for equal sets and reps.

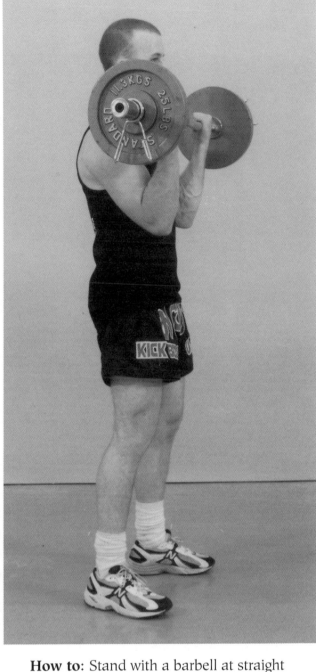

BICEPS CURL

The biceps curl—done with a barbell, dumbbells, or a cable—isolates stress on the biceps, brachialis, and forearm flexors. The biceps are used in hooks and uppercuts and are isometrically contracted to keep the arms bent. The forearms must be well conditioned due to the repetitive impact of delivering punches.

How to: Stand with a barbell at straight arm's length, knees slightly bent, back straight, abs tight, and elbows in close to the body. Keeping the elbows in, slowly bend your arms and, without leaning back, bring the bar up until your elbows are fully flexed. If you find it hard to do the standing curl without leaning back, perform the exercise with your back against the wall, remembering to keep your knees bent.

CONCENTRATION CURL

The seated concentration biceps curl isolates stress on the biceps, brachialis, and forearm flexors. The biceps are used in hooks and uppercuts and are isometrically contracted to keep the arms bent. The forearms must be well conditioned to stand up to the repetitive impact of delivering punches.

How to: Sit at the end of a bench or chair with your feet spread apart. Grasp a dumbbell with one hand and rest the back of that arm against the inside of your thigh. Bend your free arm and brace your working elbow with it as shown. With your arm straightened, slowly bend the arm to curl the weight up to the shoulder and back down slowly. Repeat for an equal number of sets and reps with the other arm.

HAMMER CURL

Hammer curls stress the brachialis and forearms in addition to the biceps. This exercise is specific to boxing because the hand position used is similar to the one used in boxing (palms facing each other). The biceps are used in hooks and uppercuts and are isometrically contracted to keep the arms bent. The forearms must be well conditioned to handle the repetitive impact of delivering punches.

How to: Stand with a pair of dumbbells at straight arm's length, knees slightly bent, back straight, abs tight, and elbows in close to the body. Keep the palms facing in toward your sides throughout the exercise. With the elbows in, slowly bend your arms and, without leaning back, bring the dumbbells up until your elbows are fully flexed. If you find it hard to do the standing curl without leaning back, perform the exercise with your back against the wall, remembering to keep your knees bent.

WRIST ROLLER

The wrist roller can be made with a piece of PVC or iron pipe, strong rope, and a weight plate. Securely fasten the rope to the pipe and secure the weight plate to the other end of the rope.

This exercise can be done with palms up or down to shift the stress to the forearm flexors or extensors. The forearms must be well conditioned to handle the repetitive impact of delivering punches.

How to: From a standing barbell curl position, simply roll your hands up toward your forearms until you run out of rope, and lower the weight under control the opposite way. (Repeat this exercise with the palms down for the forearm extensors.)

NECK DEVELOPER

Depending on how you wear the head strap, you can develop all the major muscles of your neck using this movement. A well-conditioned neck can help prevent injury in contact sports. Look at wrestlers, boxers, and UFC competitors and you will see athletes who take tremendous time on neck development!

How to: Load a light weight on the chain and wear the headdress so that the weight hangs in front of your body. Rest your hands on your thighs to support your torso in a forward lean position. Lower your chin toward your chest. Move your head to the rear as far as you can without moving your torso. Return to the starting position and repeat.

WEIGHT TRAINING ROUTINES

Split Routines

A split routine divides up the muscle groups so that the whole body is trained once over the course of a week. Each muscle group can be worked hard because it has a week to recover. The workouts are also short in duration due to the low overall workload.

After warming up with shadowboxing, pick one or two exercises per muscle group and do one to five sets per exercise. The rep ranges and weights you select will vary depending on your goals and experience. When you are finished, cool down with more shadowboxing. An example of a good basic split routine is as follows:

Workout 1	Sample Exercises	Rep Ranges
Chest	Bench press, incline press, flys	Power: 1-4
Shoulders	Seated press, rear deltoid, lateral and front raise	Size: 6-8
Triceps	Pushdowns, bench dips, kickbacks, presses	Size and strength: 8-12
Abdominals	Crunch, leg raise, folds, sit-ups	Muscle endurance: 12 +

Workout 2	Sample Exercises	Rep Ranges
Legs	Squat, leg curl and extension, stiff-leg deadlift	Size 6-8
Abdominals	Crunch, leg raise, folds, sit-ups	Size and strength 8-12
Neck	Neck harness, bridges, partner neck-up	Muscle endurance 12+

Workout 3	Sample Exercises	Rep Ranges
Back	Deadlift, row, pulldown, power clean	Power: 1-4
Biceps	EZ bar curls, hammer curls	Size: 6-8
Forearms	Wrist roller, wrist curl, power clean	Size and strength: 8-12
Abdominals	Crunch, leg raise, folds, sit-ups	Muscle endurance: 12+

SAMPLE SPLIT ROUTINE

Day 1

Exercise	Sets x reps
Chin-ups	3 x maximum
Deadlifts	3 x 6-10
Wide-grip pulldowns	3 x 8-10
(supersetted with biceps curls	3 x 8-10)
Roman chair hyperextensions	3 x 15-20
(supersetted with Roman chair crunches	3 x 15-20)
5-10 minute stretch	

Day 2

Exercise	Sets x reps
Leg extensions	3 x 8-12
(supersetted with leg curls	3 x 8-12)
Squats	3 x 6-10
	1 x 20
Stiff-leg deadlifts (medium weight)	3 x 10-12
Toe raises	3 x 15
50 crunches	
5-10 minute stretch	

Day 3

Exercise	Sets x reps
Incline presses	3 x 6-10
Bench flys	3 x 8-12
Dumbbell presses	3 x 8-10
(supersetted with dumbbell lateral raises	3 x 10-12)
Triceps skull crushers or pushdowns (medium weight)	3 x 10-12
50 crunches/5-10 minute stretch	

Abbreviated Routine

An abbreviated weight training routine is one that focuses on three or four compound core exercises. Abbreviated workouts maximize your time and should be completed in 45 minutes or less. There are not many sets involved and maximum effort should be put in to each set (one or two warm-up sets are needed but not listed). Also note that abbreviated routines are designed for increasing overall power and strength and utilize compound exercises.

VERSION 1

Day 1

Exercise	Sets x reps
Deadlifts	2 x 8-10
	2 x 4-6
Bench presses	2 x 8-10
	2 x 4-6
Chin-ups	3 x maximum (working up to 10)
Crunches	4 x 25

Day 2

Exercise	Sets x reps
Squats	2 x 8-10
	1 x 20
Stiff-leg deadlifts	3 x 10-12
Seated shoulder presses	3 x 8-10
Folds	4 x 10-25

VERSION 2

Day 1

Exercise	Sets x reps
Squats	2 x 8-10
	1 x 20
Bench or incline presses	2 x 8-10 reps
	2 x 4-6
	1 x 12-15
Crunches	1 x 30-50

Day 2

Exercise	Sets x reps
Deadlifts	2 x 8-10
	2 x 4-6
Pulldowns or bent rows	2 x 8-10
	2 x 6-8
Crunches	1 x 30-50

BASIC FULL-BODY ROUTINE

The full-body routine works all the major muscle groups in one session. The full-body workout can be used once or twice a week. The workout should take approximately one hour to complete. The idea is to pick one lift per major muscle group for three sets following warm-up. Listed below is a pair of sample routines.

VERSION 1

Exercise	Sets x reps
Leg extensions	3 x 8-10
Leg curls	3 x 8-10
Bent rows	3 x 8-10
Incline presses	3 x 8-10
Dumbbell side lateral raises	3 x 10-12
Triceps pushdowns	3 x 10-12
Dumbbell curls	3 x 10-12
Sit-ups	3 x 25-30

VERSION 2

Exercise	Sets x reps
Squats	3 x 10-12
Leg curls	3 x 10-12
Dumbbell bench presses	3 x 10-12
Pulldowns	3 x 10-12
Power cleans and presses	3 x 10-12
Barbell curls	3 x 10-12
Dumbbell triceps kickbacks	3 x 10-12
Sit-ups	3 x 25-30

CIRCUIT TRAINING

Circuit training is designed to improve muscular endurance, and it can also improve aerobic capacity if done properly. Instead of allowing the usual one to three minute's rest in between sets, move from one exercise to the next as fast as possible, only resting for a couple of minutes after the entire program has been completed once. Some variations of circuit training routines will substitute counting repetitions for lifting for a set time period, say 15 to 30 seconds. Regardless of whether you count reps or lift for a set amount of time, repeat the program two or three times in a row. Also note that unlike other routines this one includes some aerobic work after each cycle of lifts. This method is best to use with weight-training machines but can be used with free weights.

Sample Circuit Workout

Exercise	Sets x reps
Leg extension	1 x 12-15
Leg curl	1 x 12-15
Seated leg press	1 x 12 –15
Pulldown	1 x 12-15

Exercise	Sets x reps
Chest presses	1 x 12-15
Seated shoulder presses	1 x 12-15
Triceps pushdowns	1 x 12-15
Biceps curls	1 x 12-15
Incline sit-ups	1 x 20-30
Jogging/stationary cycling	10 minutes

Repeat after a brief rest period.

MUSCULAR ENDURANCE ROUTINE

This program uses high repetitions (20 to 25) and supersets to target specific muscles used heavily in combat sports. Also note that bench presses should be done with dumbbells and with the palms facing the body and rotating forward, just like the motion of a straight punch. Each exercise should be done for four or five sets with only a minute in between supersets. This routine should be combined with some aerobic conditioning and done two times per week.

Curls and pushdowns	20-24 reps/4 sets
Dumbbell bench press and dumbbell rows	20-24 reps/4 sets
Dips and folds	20-24 reps/4 sets
Hammer curls and shrugs	20-24 reps/4 sets

• • •

1. In medical terms, holding one's breath and exerting one's self is known as Valsalva's maneuver. The maneuver causes blood to be trapped in the great veins, preventing it from entering the chest and right atrium. When the breath is released, the pressure inside the chest drops and the trapped blood is quickly propelled through the heart, leading to an increase in the heart rate and blood pressure. It can bring about cardiac arrest in some cases.

CHAPTER 8
Aerobic Training

For fighters, it's not always what you know, it's what you can apply. There are times in the ring when you know exactly what to do but your body is out of gas. That is when physical conditioning comes into play. Successful Muay Thai and combat training demands that you develop both *anaerobic* (without oxygen) and *aerobic* (with oxygen) conditioning.

Anaerobic training includes high-intensity, short-duration exercise such as weight training, bag rounds, or sprinting. Anaerobic training is so intense that it exceeds the body's aerobic capacity and builds up an oxygen debt. In a fight, an opponent may show fatigue by dropping his guard or wobbling. When this happens, an experienced fighter will explode with an intense attack to try to finish off the opponent and win the fight. To have the capability for this burst of offensive power, the fighter must possess a strong anaerobic capacity.

To go the distance, athletes also need to have a great aerobic capacity. Aerobic exercise is long-lasting, low-intensity exercise that can be carried on within the body's ability to consume and process enough oxygen to support the exercise. Aerobic training increases the strength and effectiveness of the heart and lungs and disciplines the mind. In addition, regular aerobic training will improve your

recovery time between rounds. Jogging, swimming, cycling, and distance running are examples of aerobic exercise.

For centuries Thai boxers have been religious practitioners of distance running. In training camps today it is common practice to get up early in the morning and run a brisk five to seven miles before beginning the day's training. We will detail some basics of

Triathlete Tara Romano and fighter Chad Boykin do some running for aerobic conditioning, stamina, and improved recovery time.

running, beginner routines, and some advanced training methods for fighters or those with some experience.

RUNNING GEAR

Running is a great exercise to condition the heart, lungs, and legs without breaking the bank account. All the gear you really need is a good pair of running shoes. The flat boxing shoes you wear in the gym will wreak havoc on your feet and ankles should you try to run in them (and I have). Running shoes should be flexible, with good ankle support. You should not feel your foot slide around a lot inside the shoe, as good support is key.

RUNNING TECHNIQUES

To those who haven't learned to enjoy it, the misery of distance running can cause them to jog with their heads down, eyes on the ground. This is a dangerous practice because it throws off your upper body posture and leads to upper back and neck pain. Run with your head up and eyes straight ahead. Keep your shoulders relaxed, chest open, and abdominal muscles tight. Back and hip pain can result from excessively arching the back, so maintain a neutral posture. Let the arms swing forward and backward (instead of letting them cross the body) and keep them close to the body. Lift your front knee and straighten your back leg as you develop a steady, comfortable stride. Push off from the ball of your foot and land on your heel, rolling through the length of your foot. Avoid running flatfooted and pounding your feet on the ground with each step. Make a constant effort to control your breathing patterns as you go. Set your own pace.

BEGINNING RUNNING PROGRAM

For someone who has never experienced aerobic conditioning, it is best to begin with an easy workout and progress over time to a more difficult program. Walking, jogging, and running are the three progressive stages of aerobic conditioning.

- *Walking* at a fast pace is a beginner-level aerobic activity.
- *Jogging* is an intermediate-level activity and involves slow running.
- *Running* is the most advanced of the three aerobic activities but should not be mistaken for sprinting.

Beginners should start with an interval program consisting of fast walking and jogging. After several weeks of walk/jog intervals have been accomplished, one can progress to a program of jogging. And finally, after enough aerobic endurance has been attained, a program of regular running should be taken up. Faster running speeds and longer distances can always be training goals once you are conditioned from regular running. A natural sequence of progressive aerobic training is outlined below:

- Walk/jog intervals: Walk 50 yards, jog 50 yards; repeat 10 to 20 times. Over time, gradually increase the jogging interval to two or more miles.
- Jogging: Gradually increase jogging time to desired amount or jogging distance to desired goal.
- Running: As jogging endurance improves, increase your stride frequency and stride length to a comfortable running style.

If you feel you are at an intermediate level, begin jogging and go for 15 minutes, three times per week. Each run, add one minute to your jog time. Work until you can go for 60 minutes. Remember, this is not a hard run; you only need to jog at a steady pace for the determined time.

Long Runs
Once a month, attempt one run that is longer than usual. For many people, 80 to 90 minutes is a good goal. The object here is only to continue increasing your aerobic capacity, so aim for moderate and reachable increases in distance or duration.

Interval Training
To improve your speed, run at your normal pace for a set period of time or distance, then

run hard for a short period of time. Repeat this cycle for the duration of your run. A beginning interval program would have you walk for five minutes and jog for two to five minutes, continuing for 20, 30, or 60 minutes. Work your way from two-minute intervals to five, and from 20-minute workouts to 60. An intermediate example on a quarter-mile track is to run one lap at your regular pace and then run as fast as you can for the next. Continue in this manner until you have reached your target number of miles or minutes. Advanced runners can add longer, more intense interval times to the previous workout. Interval training can also be used for other aerobic activities such as cycling.

Fartlek Training

Fartlek is a Swedish word that means speed play, and is another means of aerobic conditioning. Fartlek training is the same as interval training, except that no predetermined distances are set for the hard part of the run. Interval work is done whenever you want during the run and for whatever duration you feel like doing.

Tempo Training

Tempo training involves running at a moderate pace for a set distance or time early in the run, going for a faster pace in the middle of the workout, then returning to the initial pace through to the finish. For example, run at a moderate pace for 20 minutes then pick up the pace for 25 minutes and return to the moderate pace for the final 15 minutes. This is a good method for improving running speed and aerobic conditioning.

Fight Conditioning

You want to make your training as sport-specific as possible. A fight will require bursts of high-intensity effort, while staying busy for the duration of the fight. Work up to jogging three to five miles twice per week at a steady pace. After a brief rest, perform a series of 10-, 50-, and 100-yard wind sprints with a one-minute rest in between sprints. A sprint is a short-distance all-out-effort run. Start out doing one set of sprints and add one every three weeks until you are up

to doing as many sets of sprints as there are rounds in your fight. Wind sprints can also be done after a boxing workout to improve recovery time and maximize your anaerobic threshold.

Cooldown and Stretching

It is especially important to end aerobic training with a light cooldown and at least five minutes of stretching. The cooldown serves to lower the heart rate slowly, which helps you avoid dizziness and lightheadedness. Stretching will help to prevent post-workout stiffness. Stretching after a workout is also the most effective time to stretch; while the internal temperature of the muscles is elevated, the muscles will be more responsive to the elongation of the stretch.

DETERMINE YOUR INTENSITY

To estimate how hard your heart is working during exercise, it is recommended that you monitor your heart rate. First you must determine your *maximum heart rate* and, from there, determine your *target heart rate*.

You monitor your heart rate by checking your pulse. Check your pulse at the wrist (radial) or neck (carotid) by placing two fingers on either site. (It is not recommended that you monitor your pulse with your thumb, as you have a faint pulse located in the thumb, and this can interfere with getting an accurate read.) To test the radial pulse, place two fingers on the wrist at the base of the thumb, applying steady pressure until you get a bead on the pulse. To use the carotid pulse, place two fingertips on the neck, just to the side of the larynx on the right side, applying steady pressure until you feel the pulse. To quickly assess your pulse rate, use a clock or stopwatch and count the pulse beats for 15 seconds, then multiply that number by four to estimate your heart's BPM (beats per minute).

Knowing your BPM is a valuable tool to help you assess your intensity level, but how do you know what the appropriate intensity level is?

Use the formula *220 minus your age* to determine your maximum heart rate (MHR). This is the absolute highest your heart should be working; more than this is dangerous to your health. Should you feel your heart is overworking or you have determined your heart rate is over the maximum, *do not stop exercising immediately*, but walk slowly and let your heartbeat slow down gradually to an acceptable level. Now that you know your MHR, you can determine your target heart rate.

Your target heart rate will be a percentage of your MHR and will depend on what intensity level you want to achieve. For aerobic conditioning you will want to work at a steady percentage of MHR; this can be from 60 to 75 percent. While doing anaerobic conditioning (weights, sprinting, bag intervals, or heavy sparring), you will have short, intense bursts of energy bringing your heart rate up to 75 to 95 percent of MHR; however, you will not maintain this intensity level due to the necessary rest periods. Use the formula (220 minus your age) x (.80 or 80 percent) to determine your target heart rate if you are going for 80 percent of MHR. If you are 20 years old and your MHR is 200, multiply that by the percentage of MHR you want to train at—for example, 80 percent to get a target heart rate of 160. So if you are running and want to work for 20 minutes at 80 percent MHR, monitor your heart rate and when you reach the target of 160 BPM, maintain that for the 20 minutes, then cool down.

Another way of gauging the intensity of a workout is the rating of perceived exertion (RPE). This is a less scientific but easy and reliable method of determining intensity. Simply estimate how hard your body is working by using a scale of 1 to 10 (1 being the easiest and 10 being the most difficult):

0	Nothing at all
1	Very weak
2	Weak
3	Moderate
4	Somewhat strong
5, 6	Strong
7, 8, 9	Very strong
10	Very strong, maximal[1]

1. Borg, G.V. (1982). Psychological basis of perceived exertion. Medicine and Science in Sports and Exercise, 14, 377 – 381. American College of Sports Medicine.

CHAPTER 9

Stretching

Flexibility is defined as "a joint's ability to move freely in every direction or, more specifically, through a full and normal range of motion."[1] Regular stretching is vital for increased physical performance and health in general. Weight training can leave your joints stiff and tense if flexibility training is ignored. To avoid wasting energy and to attain full power, good kickboxing technique requires your body to be relaxed and loose. Stretching regularly helps to attain this by helping the muscles relax. Stretching a muscle regularly after a workout can increase that muscle's power by an estimated 11 percent. Other benefits of stretching include:

- Reducing your chance of injury in training
- Decreasing the risk of low back pain
- Lowering stress
- Increasing blood supply to the muscles
- Increasing physical efficiency and performance

STRETCHING TECHNIQUES

Static Stretching

Static stretching is a low-intensity, long-duration (15 to 30 seconds) stretch that involves a slow and gradual elongation of the muscle. This form of stretching involves no ballistic movement and is the safest form.

Simply perform the desired stretch and gradually ease into it, holding the position when you feel a little discomfort.

Ballistic Stretching

Ballistic stretching requires a short-duration, high-force bouncing movement. Ballistic stretching is recommended only for those with a sport-specific need for the ability to withstand violent movements (as occur in basketball, wrestling, boxing). This is due to the higher risk involved in the rapid movements and forceful bouncing during the stretches. Supervised ballistic stretching can be beneficial. In fighting and training violent movements occur, thus this form of stretching prepares the muscles for the kind of high-speed and explosive movements it will perform. When you have held a static stretch for a few seconds, bounce into it and back out repeatedly.

Proprioceptive Neuromuscular Facilitation (PNF)

PNF is a stretching technique developed by doctors and physical therapists for use in physical rehabilitation. The PNF method requires an initial isometric muscle contraction for approximately five seconds, followed by relaxation and a slow, static stretch. This is known as the contract-relax stretch and should be done with a partner while under qualified supervision. For example, if you are stretching the hamstrings, tighten them for a few seconds, then relax the muscle momentarily, and finish by stretching them with a slow but steady application of pressure.

Application

Ideally, allow yourself five to 10 minutes to stretch following a warm-up, and another five to 10 minutes following your training. The timing is important because warming up increases your core body temperature, improves circulation, and allows a much safer and more productive stretch, and after-training stretching will help to eliminate waste products in your muscles caused by exercise, minimizing your morning-after soreness. Following are some good basic stretches that can be implemented in your workouts. Pick out a couple of stretches for each muscle group.

Groin Stretches

Wishbone. Sit facing a training partner with your legs straight and spread out in a "V." Grasp hands with your partner and straighten your back, sliding your pelvis forward. Have your partner place his/her feet into the inside of your ankles; as they slide forward they will straighten their legs and push their feet forward, thereby spreading your legs apart. Lean forward, and try to relax and hold this stretch for 15 to 30 seconds, gradually having your partner push a little more every few seconds.

Butterfly. Sitting erect with the soles of the feet together, gently pull your heels toward your groin and press the insides of your knees toward the floor with your elbows. You can begin by bouncing the knees up and down and then easing into a static stretch.

The butterfly is a great hip and groin stretch.

Split. Stand erect, toes pointing forward. Slowly lower your shoulders, bending at the waist, as you slide your feet out into a split as deep as you can. When you are as low as you can get, let your weight push your hips down and lower the shoulders so that they are at the same level as your hips. Hold for 20 to 30 seconds.

Chad Boykin stretches out Mike Walley in the wishbone.

Kickboxer Mike Walley demonstrates the split with amazing flexibility.

The Big Hurt. Beginning on all fours, slowly sink your hips straight down as you let your knees spread outward (similar to a split), as you lower your shoulders at or below the level of your hips. Hold for 20 to 30 seconds.

It's not called the big hurt for nothing.

Seated Split. Begin seated with both legs spread as wide as possible. Bend at the waist to first the right and then the left side, then straight down the middle. Hold each stretch for 15 to 20 seconds.

The seated split.

Hamstring Stretches
Single Leg (with partner). Stand erect with your back against a wall and one foot on the shoulder of a stooping partner. Your training partner will stand slowly, extending your straight leg as high as possible. In addition, have your partner push the ball of your foot back toward your shin to stretch the calves. Hold for 20 to 30 seconds and repeat on the other leg.

Use a partner to push you on this one.

Single Leg. Stand in front of a low step or bench and place your right foot on it. Placing your hands on your right leg for support, bend the left knee, lower yourself, and lean forward from the hips until you feel a stretch in the back of your right leg. Hold the stretch for 15 to 20 seconds and repeat on the left leg.

Hurdler Stretch. Bend one leg and put it behind you while extending the other leg on the floor. Lean forward and hold for 30 seconds, then lean backward and hold for 30 seconds. Repeat on both sides.

The hurdler stretch.

Quadriceps Stretches

Single Leg. Using a wall or chair as support, reach back and grasp the top of your right foot with your left hand. Make sure that your hips are forward and your knees are adjacent to each other. Hold the stretch for 15 to 20 seconds and repeat on the opposite leg.

Lean into the straight leg for a good hamstring stretch.

Figure Four. Sit on the floor with your left leg bent so that the foot is touching the inside of the right thigh, while the right leg is straight. Slowly lean forward, reaching for the right foot. Push ahead from the lower back and do not round the back, but keep it straight as you lean forward. Hold the stretch for 15 to 20 seconds and repeat on the right leg.

The figure four.

The single-leg quadriceps stretch.

Double Leg. Begin by kneeling on both shins. Slowly bend backward, keeping your knees forward, shins in contact with the floor. Hold for 15 to 20 seconds.

Mike Walley shows advanced flexibility on the double-leg quad stretch.

Outer Hip Stretches

Seated Figure Four. Sit erect on a bench or chair. Bend your left knee, placing your left foot on the right knee. Keeping your back straight, bend at the waist and lean forward at the hips while pushing down slightly on the left knee. Hold the stretch for 15 to 20 seconds and repeat on both sides.

Lean into the bent leg for a deep outer hip stretch.

Hip Roll. While seated, cross your left foot over your straight right leg, left knee bent. Use your arm to pull your knee toward your chest as you turn your lower back in the opposite direction. Hold the stretch for 15 to 20 seconds and repeat on the opposite leg.

The hip roll.

Lying Hip Roll. Lying on your back, bend your right knee, pulling it across your body and toward your left shoulder. This stretch can be made most effective with the help of a training partner, who can use some body weight to push your knee around the hip while holding down the opposite shoulder. Hold the stretch for 15 to 30 seconds and repeat on the opposite leg.

The lying hip roll.

Calf Stretches
Wall Stretch. Using a wall as support, place one foot behind the other. Bend the front knee slightly and straighten the back leg with the heel on the floor. Lean forward from the hips. Hold the stretch for 15 to 20 seconds and repeat on the opposite leg.

Shin Stretch. Using a wall as support, place one foot behind the other. Bend the front knee slightly, and straighten the back leg with the top of the foot (toes) on the floor, lean the hips forward. Hold the stretch for 15 to 20 seconds and repeat on the opposite leg.

Bend the foot to stretch the calf muscles.

Reverse the foot position to stretch the dorsi flexors (shin muscles).

Back Stretches

Mid-Back Roll. While lying on your back, bend and lift one knee, pulling it toward your chest. Keep your back in contact with the floor at all times. Hold the stretch for 15 to 20 seconds.

Roll the lower back and hip.

Cat Stretch. On hands and knees, roll your back down while lifting your head up. Then round the mid-back, arching it as you lower your head.

The cat stretch will stretch the mid-back.

Upper Lat Stretch. Lock wrists with a partner. Both of you will be in a squatting position, knees bent, hips low. Slowly stand up together while leaning your weight backward, "pulling" each other, until you are both standing.

Stretch the upper back with a partner. Keep your weight back and arms straight.

Abdominal Stretch

Ab Stretch. Lying on your stomach, place your hands in a push-up position. Lift your upper body, keeping the hips and legs on the floor. Hold for 15 to 20 seconds.

The abdominal stretch.

Chest Stretch
Chest and Shoulder Stretch. Stand and place your right hand against a wall. Rotate your torso away from the hand until you feel a stretch in the chest and shoulder. Hold for 15 to 20 seconds and repeat on the opposite side.

Shoulder Stretches
Rear Shoulder Stretch. With shoulders down and relaxed, bring your right arm across your chest, parallel to the floor. Place your left hand on the upper arm and apply gentle pressure toward the body. Hold for 15 seconds and repeat on the left side.

Grasp a wall or have a partner bring your arms back to stretch your chest.

The shoulder and trapezius stretch.

Towel Stretch. Grasp a long, rolled towel on each end and stand erect with your arms straight and the towel resting on your upper thighs. Move the towel upward and backward overhead, allowing the towel to rest on the backs of your thighs. Return to the start and repeat five to eight times.

Triceps Stretch
Elbow Bends. Bend your right elbow and use your left arm to bring the bent elbow up and behind your head until you feel a stretch in the triceps of the bent arm. Hold for 10 seconds and repeat on the opposite side.

The towel stretch, start.

Bend the elbow for a triceps stretch.

Forearm Stretch
Wrist Bend. Place your palms flat on the floor, fingers pointing toward you, and lean forward with your arms straightened, weight on your forearms. Bridge up to stretch the entire body. Hold for 20 to 30 seconds and repeat.

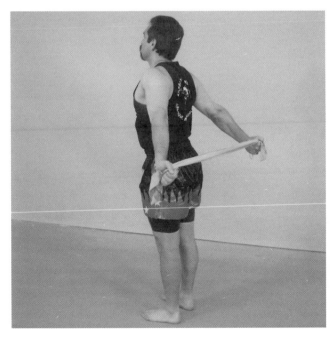

The towel stretch, finish.

Bridge up with the palms on the mat for the forearm stretch.

Neck Stretch

Neck Roll. Use your hand to gently pull your head forward and to either side to stretch the muscles of the neck and upper back.

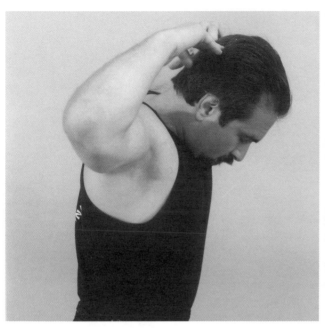

Stretch the neck front to back.

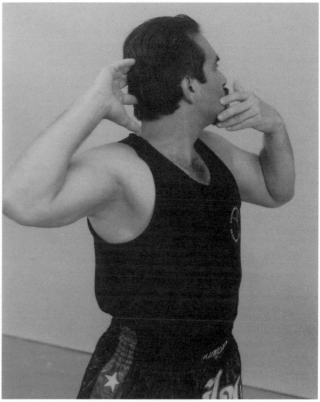

Stretch the neck side to side.

1.   Cotton, Richard T. *Personal Trainer Manual.* San Diego, CA: American Council on Exercise, 1996.

CHAPTER 10

Goal Setting

Whether you are aspiring to be a fighter, to get in shape, or to learn to defend yourself, it is important to set goals. Very few people begin training without some goal in mind. Short-term goals provide you with specific, easy-to-reach objectives that you plan to accomplish over a set amount of time. They should be progressive and easy to achieve. A long-term goal may take several months or years to attain. For example, if you haven't done any exercise in years, you can't reasonably expect to be able to run five miles, bench press 200 pounds, and fight a three-round match right away. These specific goals would be long-term. Meanwhile you can set reachable short-term goals such as: *In the next eight weeks I will run 10 minutes twice a week and train in boxing twice a week.* After the eight weeks is up you can evaluate your progress and increase the training a little. In this example you could add 45 minutes of weight training per week, and aim to lose two or three percent body fat (assuming you are overweight to begin with) within the next eight or 10 weeks.

For health reasons, it is typically better to aim for losing body fat percentages or inches around the gut than it is to aim for losing weight. That is because with weight training (and even bag work), your body will likely be putting on muscle, which weighs much more than fat.

Thus, you could be losing fat yet maintaining or even gaining weight. Simply losing pounds could mean you're losing water weight or even muscle tissue if you are not eating properly.

In the case of a competitive fighter, however, it may be necessary to be at a certain weight in order to make a weight class. You must keep this in mind as you design your training program. Generally speaking, fighters try to be at the high end of a weight class in order to have a strength and weight advantage over the competition.

Whether you are setting short-term or long-term goals, you want to make them specific, measurable, attainable, and time-bound.

Specific. The goals "I want to get in shape" and "I want to be able to fight" are not specific. Clearly define your objectives and they are more likely to be met. "I want to lose 15 pounds" and "I want to be able to spar anyone in the gym and hold my own" are better alternatives.

Measurable. "I want to lose 10 percent body fat in three months" is a measurable goal. With measurable goals there can be no question of whether the goal was achieved.

Attainable. If you have never lifted weights before, it is unreasonable to expect that you will break the world record in the deadlift in six months. You should set your goals as challenging, but reachable. A goal that is too easy won't get you off the couch, and one that is too hard will likely put you back on the couch from frustration.

Time-bound. You will want to set specific deadlines for the completion of each goal you set. Putting a deadline on your goal will create a sense of urgency. Procrastination will always be your worst enemy.

Another helpful practice to adopt in achieving your goals is the use of a training journal. A journal will list the time, intensity, type, and duration of your training. Other notes, such as the date, time, diet, and sleep (or lack thereof) can prove helpful. On the next page is a journal with sample entries. Following that is a blank training journal that you can photocopy and put into a notebook for your own use.

Lastly, it is important to note that with fighting, or even getting yourself in shape, you have no one but yourself to credit for your success or blame for your losses. Unlike being a player on a football team, you can't blame your defensive team or your injured quarterback if you lose a game. The only one left in the locker room is you. This is motivating for some and scary for others. You are your own team, and setting goals is a big weapon in your arsenal, no matter what your ultimate objective.

DAY/MONTH/YEAR:

Training Type	Description (Duration, Sets/Reps/Weight/Rounds)	Notes (Heart Rate, Intensity, Mood, Diet)
Tuesday: Thai boxing	3 rounds shadowboxing/5 min. abdominal work, 5 rounds Thai pads, 5 rounds sparring	HR 180 BPM. Level 8 intensity
Wednesday: Weight training	Bench presses: 3 x 10 x 175 lbs. Dumbbell shoulder presses: 3 x 12 x 55 lbs. Triceps pushdowns: 4 x 12 x 75 lbs. Crunches: 5 x 25. Shadowboxing 3 rounds.	Stretching 15 minutes. Took one-minute rest between sets.
Thursday: Running, Thai boxing	Jogged 3 miles in a.m./ran four wind sprints of 50 yards. 5 rounds of bag work. 3 rounds sparring/100 kicks on bag	Felt tired in afternoon.
Friday: Weight training	Deadlifts: 3 x 8 x 210 lbs. Chin-ups: 4 x 8. Dumbbell curls: 4 x 12 x 30 lbs. Jackknives: 4 x 25.	Took two minutes' rest between sets. Workout took 40 minutes w/stretching.
Saturday: Thai boxing	Focus mitts: 3 rounds. Thai pads: Knees/ Kicks 3 rounds. Touch sparring: 6 rounds. 10-minute stretch.	HR 170 BPM. Workout felt easy, was a 6.

DAY/MONTH/YEAR:

Training Type	Description (Duration, Sets/Reps/Weight/Rounds)	Notes (Heart Rate, Intensity, Mood, Diet)

Conclusion

If the goal of your martial arts training is to learn real-world stand-up combat skills, then Thai boxing is for you. The advantages of Muay Thai are in the actual application of the art and the realism of its training methods. Thai boxing as a sport has virtually no rules; full-power strikes are allowed to every part of the body, using every weapon of the body! The majority of martial arts that have enjoyed popularity in the United States test their athletes in "point sparring tournaments," which impose rigid rules regarding the nature of physical contact. Many kickboxers fight in the ring under rules that outlaw kicks to the leg, knee strikes, and elbow strikes. Unfortunately, in the street the idiot who wants to test his manhood at your expense, or the monster that wants to rape, rob, or brutalize you will not adhere to any rules. He probably will not be impressed with your black belt or philosophical knowledge of martial arts either.

Compared to other stand-up combat sports, Thai boxing also employs the most practical methods of training other than boxing, which uses only the hands as weapons. Fighting requires hard physical conditioning, full-power strikes, and regular contact sparring. Training provides these components and challenges one's mental toughness. Specialized equipment is used to practice hitting with full speed and power while defending yourself from the constant attack of your training partner, simulating the intensity of a real fight. In sparring, you take many punches and kicks as well as deliver them. Many people can hit hard, but the ability to take a hit is what separates the wannabes from those who are truly prepared for combat (be it voluntary combat or self-defense). The knowledge of the art must be proven in the ring. This experience gained "the hard way" cannot be compensated for by any other method. There are no katas or preconceived hypothetical assumptions of what will work in any given fight.

Muay Thai is a powerful means of combat that can bring confidence, conditioning, strength, and toughness to anyone, from dedicated fighters to everyday men, women, and children. It is an art that requires the discipline to push your body farther than you have before. Thai boxing is a tool used to reach your goals, whether you want to compete in the ring, defend yourself, improve your physical conditioning, or just have a positive and challenging hobby. The rewards of confidence and self-discipline carry over to every other aspect of life. No matter how many years you put into training, there is always something new to learn, and new challenges to face.

Over the years I have seen all kinds of people enjoy training in this tough sport. A longtime member of my gym began training with us in his late forties and had done no other exercise in his life! He has made tremendous progress and still trains to this day, healthier than ever. One female student decided to begin training after having to fight off an assailant while working in a foreign country. And one of the most dedicated and sharpest boxers I have ever trained had his first kickboxing match after only six months of hard training. I personally had to face the challenge of training and fighting as a diabetic, requiring multiple insulin injections and blood tests each day. Despite your challenges or obstacles, if you have a determined mind, your possibilities, rewards, potential, and future are unlimited!

I hope this book will be a valuable reference manual of training information, techniques, ideas, and programs. This manual was aimed at novices or folks who may be interested in self-defense or the sport, but don't know much about it. If you grew up in Thailand or already have a fight record, then there was nothing too new here. If you have enjoyed the information and ideas in this book, please recommend it to friends (or people you hate, I don't care. If, however, *you* hate it, well, let's just keep that between us). Following the conclusion there will be a listing of additional combat sport resources that are available to you, including gyms, Web sites, equipment manufacturers, trainers, and organizations.

"A workout is 25 percent perspiration and 75 percent determination. Stated another way, it is one part physical exertion and three parts self-discipline. Doing it is easy once you get started. A workout makes you better today than you were yesterday. It strengthens the body, relaxes the mind, and toughens the spirit. When you work out regularly, your problems diminish and your confidence grows. A workout is a personal triumph over laziness and procrastination. It is the badge of a winner—the mark of an organized, goal-oriented person who has taken charge of his or her destiny. A workout is a wise use of time and an investment in excellence. It is a way of preparing for life's challenges and proving to yourself that you have what it takes to do what is necessary. A workout is a key that helps unlock the door to opportunity and success. Hidden within each of us is an extraordinary force. Physical and mental fitness are the triggers that can release it. A workout is a form of rebirth. When you finish a good workout, you don't simply feel better, *you feel better about yourself.*"

—George Allen
4/29/1922 – 12/31/1990
President's Council of Sports and Physical Fitness

Additional Resources

EQUIPMENT

Century Martial Arts
1705 National Boulevard
Midwest City, OK 73110
<www.centuryma.com>

Everlast Boxing
14371 West 100th Street
Lenexa, KS 66215
<www.everlastboxing.com>

Fairtex Muay Thai
444 Clementina Street
San Francisco, CA 94103
<www.fairtex.com>

FBT
845-847-847/1 Rama 6 Road
Wangmai, Patumwan
Bangkok 10330 Thailand
<www.fbtsports.com>

Macho Products, Inc.
10045 102nd Terrace, Sebastian, FL 32958
<www.macho.com>

Otomix
3691 Lenawee Avenue
Los Angeles, CA 90016
<www.otomix.com>

Revgear
11750 Roscoe Boulevard #11
Sun Valley, CA 91352
<www.innovare.com/revgear/>

Ringside
9650 Dice Lane
Lenexa, KS 66215
<www.ringside.com>

Title Boxing
14371 W. 100th Street
Building C
Lenexa, KS 66215

SANCTIONING BODIES

International Kickboxing Federation (IKF)
9385 Old State Highway
P.O. Box 1205
Newcastle, CA 95658
<www.ikfkickboxing.com>

International Sport Kickboxing Association (ISKA)
ISKA World Headquarters
P.O. Box 90147
Gainesville, FL 32607-0147
<www.iska.com>

World Kickboxing Association (WKA)
James Court
63 Gravelly Lane, Erdington,
Birmingham B23 6LX England
<www.kickboxing-wka.co.uk>

World Muay Thai Council (WMTC)
118 Viphavadee-rangsit Rd. (Soi 2)
Dindang, Bangkok 10400
<www.wmtc.nu>

INTERNET SITES

Kickboxing Unlimited:
    <www.kickboxingunlimited.com>
Paladin Press: <www.paladin-press.com>
Pop Praditbatuga's "The Belt is in the Ring":
    <http://members.aol.com/Thaiboxing2000/
    muay.html>
Master Toddy Muay Thai:
    <www.mastertoddy.com>
World Muay Thai Council:
    <www.wmtc.nu/index.html>

Bibliography

BOOKS

Rebac, Zoran. *Thai Boxing Dynamite: The Explosive Art of Muay Thai.* Boulder, CO: Paladin Press, 1987.

Grymkowski, Peter et al., *The Gold's Gym Training Encyclopedia.* Chicago: Contemporary, 1984.

Cotton, Richard T. *Personal Trainer Manual.* San Diego, CA: American Council on Exercise, 1996.

Borg, G.V. Psychological basis of perceived exertion. *Medicine and Science in Sports and Exercise,* 14, 377 – 381. American College of Sports Medicine, 1982.

Kirkley, George. *Weight Lifting and Weight Training.* New York: Bell Publishing, 1973.

Schlosberg, Suzanne. *Fitness for Dummies.* Foster, CA: IDG Books, 1996.

Karter, Karon. *The Complete Idiot's Guide to Kickboxing.* Indianapolis, IN: Alpha Books, 2000.

Shanahan, John. *The Most Brilliant Thoughts of All Time (In Two Lines or Less).* New York, New York: Harper Collins, 1999.

MAGAZINES

Wilson, Terry. "Muay Thai's Fight for Respect." *Muay Thai.* Burbank: CFW Enterprises, April 2000.

Carter, Dave. "Tradition: The Heart of Muay Thai." *Muay Thai.* Burbank: CFW Enterprises, April 2000.

Plante, Joseph. "10 Mindsets to Ring Readiness." *Muay Thai.* Burbank: CFW Enterprises, October, 2000.

Quadros, Stephen. "What Does it Take to Win the K-1?" *Inside Kung Fu* (November 1999): p. 118.

VIDEOS

Worawoot, Pud Pad Noy. Muay Thai Fighting and Training Techniques. Panther Video Productions, San Clemente, CA. <www.panthervideo.com>

Rutten, Bas. Extreme Pancrase: Fighting Fitness Workout Routine. Panther Video Productions, San Clemente, CA. <www.panthervideo.com>

INTERNET SITES

Praditbatuga, Pop. The Belt is in the Ring, <http://members.aol.com/Thaiboxing2000/muay.html>

Fox, Stephan. World Muay Thai Council Homepage, <http://www.wmtc.nu/index.html>

Wayne, C. Journal of Chinese Martial Science, <http://members.tripod.com/~crane69/index6d.htm>

About the Author

Chad Boykin is the managing co-owner of Kickboxing Unlimited in Raleigh, North Carolina (<www.kickboxingunlimited.com>), and has several years of experience in Muay Thai-style kickboxing and American boxing. In addition to being a Black Belt Martial Arts Instructor, he is an ACE and Phase II certified personal fitness trainer. He enjoys writing and has had articles published in various magazines such as *Martial Arts Legends Presents, American Diabetes Association: Forecast,* and has contributed articles to various newsletters and newspapers in North Carolina. He has an A.A.S. degree in business administration and is working on a degree in human resources.

Chad has competed in Thai boxing, boxing, and kickboxing rules fights in addition to races and weight lifting contests. In 1998, Chad won the Toughman boxing tournament via four consecutive knockouts. Earlier that year, he won the North Carolina Academy of Kickboxing middleweight amateur kickboxing title.

He feels that winning is great but that more is learned from losing and training hard in the gym. Chad is currently training in Brazilian jiu-jitsu to prepare for No Holds Barred competition.

Being hospitalized with juvenile onset diabetes at a young age taught him that anything can happen and to enjoy every day. Aside from the world of ring sports, training, and writing, he enjoys time with his family, reading, and whenever possible doing nothing at all.

"The older I get, the better I was!"